William Seward

Biographiana - By the Compiler of Anecdotes of Distinguished Persons

Vol. II

William Seward

Biographiana - By the Compiler of Anecdotes of Distinguished Persons
Vol. II

ISBN/EAN: 9783337031091

Printed in Europe, USA, Canada, Australia, Japan

Cover: Foto ©ninafisch / pixelio.de

More available books at **www.hansebooks.com**

BIOGRAPHIANA.

BY THE COMPILER

OF

ANECDOTES

OF

DISTINGUISHED PERSONS.

VOL. II.

—————VARIO DIVERSA PALATO.
HOR.

LONDON:
PRINTED FOR J. JOHNSON, ST. PAUL'S CHURCH-YARD.
M,DCC,XCIX.

BIOGRAPHIANA.

BOILEAU.

BOILEAU was one day visited by a noble and unprofessional person, who reproached him with not having returned his first visit. "You and I," said the satyrist, "are upon different terms. I lose my time when I pay a visit; you only get rid of your's when you do so." Yet when Menage called upon him one day, and, on finding him at his studies, begged his pardon for interrupting him, he replied, "Sir, one man of letters can never interrupt another."

Under the ancien regime of France, the manner of paying visits in that country was attended with no inconvenience; no time was lost, nor any interruption occasioned. Those persons that were not upon very intimate terms with each other were contented with giving in their names to the servants, who kept a visiting-book; this they called *se faire inscrire chez un tel*, and the compliment was returned in the same manner. No one can tell what the present French do in these cases, as they have in general appeared to treat each other with as little ceremony as they have done their neighbours.

ABBÉ DE ST. PIERRE.

This honest politician made the christian rule, of doing as you would be done by, apply even to politics. "The people," says he, "pay their taxes willingly, when a sove-
"reign can say to himself, Would *I*, were I
"a subject, that the sovereign should tax
"me in the same manner that I do my sub-
"jects, and that he should demand of me such
"a subsidy for such a certain purpose? They
"pay willingly," adds he, "when all persons
"in a state are taxed in proportion to their
"property, and when they know with cer-
"tainty that the money thus drawn from them
"is expended with wisdom and with proper
"economy."

"Every person," says the Abbé, in his "Tarif
"Tarifié," shall declare what he is worth,
"and shall be taxed in proportion to his pro-
"perty, of whatever kind it is. This tarif
"shall be calculated at five per cent. on the
"income of lands that the possessor keeps in
"his own hands; with respect to lands that
"are let to farm, they shall be taxed at two
"and a half per cent. to be paid by the tenant.
"The tax on money employed in trade shall be
"at one and a half per cent. The tax on
"in-

" industry and labour shall be fixed at the rate
" of so many day's work in each profession.

" The certainty," adds he, (he is speaking
of old France) " that a person shall never be
" excessively nor exclusively taxed, nor more
" taxed in proportion than his neighbours, will
" establish commerce; increase the number
" of the inhabitants of the country, the
" number of those who cultivate the ground,
" and of consequence the fruits of the earth;
" the rents and the revenues of the nobility;
" and diminish the number of the poor and
" the idle, because by these means every one
" will find some work or some occupation on
" which he may employ himself."

This benevolent projector has put the advantages of a public school over private education in a very strong light.

" Children," says he, " that are brought
" up at a public school are in general more
" manly* than those brought up at a private
" seminary; they are used to wait upon them-

* A celebrated admiral of our times, on seeing the dormitory at Westminster, exclaimed, " Were it not for this, and
" the forecastle of a man of war, our nation would become
" a country of macaronies."

" selves;

" felves; to take care of their clothes and their
" books, and to buy what they want for them-
" felves; they are taught to behave well to each
" other; to write and to keep their accounts;
" with many other habits of great ufe to them
" in their future life. Raillery is indeed a
" vice; but it often ferves to correct the
" vices of him to whom it is applied, efpe-
" cially when all his companions join in it.
" The proverb, that fays, Familiarity breeds
" contempt, is founded in truth. Yet ftill
" parents wifh that their children fhould re-
" fpect them. It is true, indeed, that a mo-
" ther wifhes often to fee her fon; but fhe
" does not confider, that the feldomer he fees
" her the more refpect he entertains for her.
" If a child in general refpects his father more
" than his mother, it is becaufe he is lefs
" cockered by one than by the other. It is odd,
" but it is too true, that the tendernefs of
" mothers, inftead of being advantageous to
" children, is too often pernicious to them;
" and that a particular child, who would have
" become a man of principle and of diligence,
" has turned out idle and worthlefs, becaufe
" he has had a bad education, and has been
" too much fondled by his mother."

M. DE

M. DE BUFFON,

if not the historian, was most assuredly the orator of nature. The magic of his style either makes you believe what he tells you to be true, or disregard whether it is so or not. He excels in description, and there is not, perhaps, in any language whatever, so eloquent a writer. He has the talent of dressing with flowers things that in many other writers would disgust, and yet are necessary to his book from the nature of his subject; and he so decorates them, that under his pen their offensiveness is not perceived. M. Herault de Sechelles, an eloquent lawyer, visited M. de Buffon some years ago, and published an account of his entertaining visit with this title, "*Voyage à Montbard en* 1785. From this book the following extracts are made: "I mentioned," says Herault de Sechelles, "the word *genius* to him—'Genius*,' replied he, 'is nothing but a strong disposition to take pains. Invention depends upon patience. A writer should

---

* "I know of no such thing as genius," said our Hogarth to Mr. Gilbert Cooper one day; "genius is nothing but labour and diligence." This definition of genius was given by a person who seemed to have the fairest claims to that gift of heaven; the greatest ethical painter that ever existed; and a painter of so exuberant a fancy that every figure in his pictures is doing something, and his

" should observe and should consider his sub-
" ject for a great while; it then unrolls itself
" and developes itself by degrees; you feel
" then as if a small stroke of electricity had
" pervaded your head, and at the same time
" made an impression upon your heart. That
" is the instant of genius; then you feel the
" pleasure of composition; a pleasure so great,
" that I have often spent twelve or fourteen
" hours together at it. It was my greatest
" enjoyment; indeed I was more absorbed
" with it than with my own fame. Fame may
" come afterwards if it pleases; and, to say
" truth, in general it does come afterwards.
" But would you increase the rapture, and at
" the same time be original, when you are
" writing on a subject open no book upon
" that subject; draw every thing from your
" own head, and do not consult a book till
" you find that you can produce nothing. I
" have always made use of this method when
" I wrote. By these means I have always en-

his canvass is never extensive enough for his ideas; so that in the ends of his pictures you often see mere hands and legs introduced for want of room for the faces that should accompany them; and which have still a propriety and a distinctiveness of action.

That honour to human nature, Sir Isaac Newton, said of himself, " that if ever he had been able to do any thing, he " had effected it by patient thinking only."

" joyed

" joyed every author that I have read. We
" become on a level with them, or above
" them: we judge them, we divine their mean-
" ing, and we read them with great rapidity.
" With respect to expression, always join the
" image to the idea. The image should al-
" ways precede the idea to prepare the mind.
" You should not always make use of the pe-
" culiar and distinctive word, which is some-
" times a common one, but you should make
" use of the word that is very near to it. A
" comparison is in general necessary to make
" the idea felt; and, to make use of a
" comparison myself, I will represent style
" under the image of a cutting out, which one
" must pare and twist about in every direction
" to give it the form required. When you
" write, attend to the first impulse of your
" mind, it is in general the best; then lay
" aside for some days, or for a considerable
" time, what you have written. Nature does
" not operate all at once; she operates by
" degrees, after having rested and taken
" additional strength. We must employ
" ourselves continually about the same thing;
" follow it up, and not occupy ourselves
" upon different objects. When I am doing
" one thing I never think of any other. In
" your profession, that of the law, it is differ-
" ent; you have often many *plaidoyers* to com-

" pare

"pare at the same time, and often on subjects
"not very important. You are pressed for
"time, you can only consult your notes; in
"that case, instead of attending to be correct,
"you must give as much as possible into the
"eloquence of words; that is in general suf-
"ficient for those persons who hear you."

M. de Buffon often said, "The style of a
"man is the man himself. Poets have no
"style, because they are fettered by the
"measure of their verses, which makes them
"slaves*. So when any one talks to me of
"the talents of a particular person, I reply,
"let me see what he has written. The style
"of M. Thomas is too elaborate, too in-
"flated; that of J. J. Rousseau is better, but
"it has all the defects of his want of edu-
"cation; it abounds too much in inter-
"jections and exclamations; he is conti-
"nually apostrophizing. With respect to
"myself," said he, "I am every day learning
"to write. I have passed fifty years at my
"writing-table; I often read over what I
"have written, and I find either ideas that I
"wish to alter, or others that I cannot make

* Malherbe (the celebrated French poet) used to say of poets, that they were of much the same use in a state as good skittle-players.

"better."

" better." He said, in speaking of Rousseau, " I was very fond of him; but when I saw his ' Confessions' I ceased to esteem him. The badness of his heart disgusted me, and the contrary of what happened to most persons happened to Rousseau in my mind; after his death he began to lose my esteem. I cannot excuse Rousseau his contradictions."

" One may say of M. Buffon," adds Sechelles, " that he calculates his thought and his expression as he calculates every thing else; a remarkable quality that he acquired from his knowledge of mathematics, and from his habit of explaining them. He said that he had studied them from early life, first in the writings of Euclid, and then in those of the Marquis de l'Hôpital. At twenty years of age," added he, " I had discovered the Binome of Newton, without knowing that it had been previously discovered by Newton." M. Sechelles asked M. Buffon how a man should form his mind; he replied, " by reading merely the capital books of every kind and on every science, because they are all related, as Cicero says; because the views of one may be applied to the views of another, though a man is not destined to exercise

" exercise them all. So for a lawyer the
" knowledge of the art military and of its
" principal operations would not be useless.
" I have always done so," added he; " but do
" not let this frighten us; the principal books
" upon every subject are but few, fifty per-
" haps at most. I recommend the reading
" only of the works of the great geniuses, of
" whom there are very few in the world, only
" five, Newton, Bacon, Leibnitz, Montes-
" quieu, and myself. With respect to Newton,
" he has discovered a great principle, but he
" passed his whole life in calculations to de-
" monstrate it; and with respect to style he
" can be of no use. He appeared to me to
" esteem Leibnitz more than Lord Bacon; he
" said that Leibnitz carried away every thing
" by the force of his genius, while Bacon's
" discoveries were the fruits of the most pro-
" found meditation; and that the real ge-
" nius of Leibnitz was not to be found in the
" complete edition of his works, but in the
" Memoirs he composed for the Academy of
" Berlin. In quoting Montesquieu he praised
" his talents, not his style. ' which,' said
" he, ' is not often good: it is too concise,
" and wants clearness. I knew the President
" well,' added he; ' the defect of his style
" arose from his physical imperfections. He

" was

"was nearly blind, and so extremely *vif*,
"that in general he forgot what he wished
"to dictate; so that he was obliged to con-
"fine himself within the narrowest space
"possible.

"M. Buffon was very anxious that I should
"go to mass on the Sunday I was with him.
"He always goes himself on that day and
"gives a Louis d'Or to the poor. His fa-
"vourite principle is, that religion should be
"respected; and that in small towns where
"a person is observed, he should give offence
"to no one in that respect. I am persuaded,'
said he, 'that in all your public speeches you
"have acted in the same manner. I have
"paid the same attention to religion in all my
"works.

* * * * * *

"Every man should pay the same respect
"to religion; those who act otherwise are
"fools. Voltaire, Diderot, and Helvetius,
"have not done so, and have brought upon
"themselves great trouble. The last was my
"intimate friend; I always advised him to be
"moderate; he was not so, and he had suffi-
"cient reason to repent of his not having fol-
"lowed my advice.' Buffon," continues
Sechelles,

Sechelles, " never takes up his pen to write
" till he has long meditated his subject, and
" has in general no paper near him but that
" on which he is writing. This, in one's
" study," adds his biographer, " is more ne-
" ceſſary than moſt writers think. The re-
" gularity, in fact, which a man ſees about
" him is communicated to his productions.
" It is ſtrongly recommended by two labo-
" rious writers, M. Necker and the Abbé
" Terrai."

A lady once told Buffon, that what
Rouſſeau had mentioned in his 'Emile' reſpecting women nurſing their own children
was not new, for that he himſelf had mentioned it long before in his writings. " I had,
" indeed, *told them* ſo," replied Buffon; " but
" Rouſſeau has *commanded* it, and muſt make
" himſelf obeyed *.

Buffon had a ſon of whom he was very
fond, and who was an idolater of his father's

---

* When Rouſſeau's 'Emile' came out, an able phyſician
ſaid, " There are many excellent truths in this book; it
" will do much ſervice to mankind; but I foreſee that our
" ladies will do much harm to their children by ſtarving
" them in two ways; by a diet compoſed too much of vege-
" table food, and by expoſing them too much to the cold."

glory and reputation. When under the fatal guillotine he exclaimed, "*Citoyens, je* "*me nomme Buffon.*"

MARSHAL BELLEISLE,

to accustom himself to contemplate that great dignity to which he arrived, or to raise in his mind that passion for glory which afterwards succeeded so well, used to walk about his room every morning exclaiming for half an hour together, " I am resolved to be a great " general, and Marshal of France."

LE COMTE DE GELIN

was implicated in the unhappy business of La Charette, and brought before the military commission. Being asked by one of his judges whether he was married or not, " I am mar- " ried," said he, " to the daughter of mine " and of your master." [He had married a natural daughter of Louis XV.] Before he was executed he exclaimed, " I die for my " God and my king."

SENECA!

SENECA

wrote some lines which he called 'The Irresolute Man;' they have been thus translated by an ingenious youth, who felt but too sensibly the ill consequences of the folly described in them:

THE IRRESOLUTE MAN.

While Jack too long deliberates
  Which lot of life 'tis best to draw,
  Or arms, or physic, church, or law,
And still his choice procrastinates;

Neglected Time with rapid wing
  In silence sweeps the listless hours,
  Each idly crops life's freshest flow'rs,
Which knows, alas! no second spring:

For soon old age with wintry hands
  Shall freeze the current of the soul,
  Her ardent energies controul,
And bind the powers in icy bands:

Yet Jack has mem'ry, taste, and wit,
  In learning prompt, in speaking ready;
  But, wav'ring, doubtful, light, unsteady,
For ev'ry state is now unfit.

While floating on each wand'ring wave
  Of passion, chance, caprice, and whim,
  Death comes and strait decides for him,
To fix his station in the grave.

The character of Aliger, so finely depicted by Dr. Johnson in 'The Rambler,' is said to have been that of the late learned Mr. Floyer Sydenham, the translator of the Dialogues of Plato.

~~~~~

FATHER GERDIL

says of education, " that it is indeed an art, " but one of those which are directory, pro- " ducing nothing apparently at the time. " The increase is most assuredly slow; the ad- " vantage not readily seen, and at a distance. " It is like the shadow of a dial which is still " going on, yet no eye sees it move." Ignorant parents do not know

M. sis quantæ est, humanam condere mentem;

how difficult and how tedious a business it is to build up the fabric of the human mind to advantage; and by their folly and precipitation, in not suffering the foundations to be laid deep and solid, not unfrequently render it a building of sand, instead of a fabric of stone; and wish to pluck the fruit from the tree before the blossom is set.

FONTENELLE

FONTENELLE

had one day drawn *The King* on the *Jour des Rois*, Twelfth-day; and being asked whether he would be a despot, answered, " A fine " question indeed!"

~~~~~

RACINE.

Every line in this poet is excellent. Voltaire says, " that a comment would be made " with great case on his Works, for that there " would be nothing more to do than to write " under every passage beautiful, sublime, ex-" quisite." Boileau used to say, " that he " had taught Racine to make verses with " difficulty. The easiest verses," adds he, " that are known, are not those which are " composed with the greatest case."

He, in conjunction with Boileau, was appointed historiographer to Louis XIV. who had once ordered him to attend him to a siege that was carrying on in Flanders. Racine, however, remained at Versailles: and when the king at his return expressed his surprise at it, and

and told him that it was by no means a journey
of any length; " Very true Sire," replied
the poet: " We had ordered our campaign
" dresses; but our taylors made us wait so
" long, that when they brought them home,
" the town your majesty went to besiege
" had been long taken.*"

Madame de Maintenon was one of Racine's
greatest protectors. He had one day represented to her in very strong terms, the miseries
which Louis the Fourteenth's expensive wars
had entailed upon his people. She was much
struck with the force of his reasons, and the
powers of his description; and desired him to
draw up for her a memorial on the subject.
This she shewed to Louis, who was much displeased at it, and insisted on knowing the author. She had the weakness to tell him, and
he immediately exclaimed, " What, because
" he knows how to write good verses, does he
" pretend to know every thing else; and be-
" cause he is a great poet, does he think him-
" self capable of being a great minister?" On
being told of this, Racine exclaimed, " I
" am a dead man," ran into his bed-chamber,

* The collections that those great men had made for the
History were burnt in a fire at M. de Valincour's house.

and took immediately to his bed, forgetting what he had advanced in his tragedy of Efther:

> What bufinefs has that man at Court,
> Who cannot many a flight fupport;
> Nor knows each feeling to beguile,
> And hide thofe griefs in many a fmile,
> Which his fad aching heart opprefs
> With ev'ry pang of wretchednefs.

He went afterwards to Court at the requeft of Madame de Maintenon, but appeared very melancholy and unhappy there, in fpite of the notice the king affected to take of him. He died foon afterwards, and told his friend Boileau, who came to fee him in his illnefs, "I love you fo much, my dear friend, that "I am really glad to die before you. I do not "know how I could have lived without you;" and in the fame ftrain of ardent friendfhip, when on his death bed he applied for the arrears of his own penfion for the fake of his family, he defired his fon to afk for thofe due to Boileau at the fame time. "We muft "never be feparated," faid he; "and I am "anxious to let him know that I conti- "nued his friend to the laft moment of "my life."

Racine

Racine was an excellent scholar. His Sophocles and Euripides were full of marginal notes on the dubious paſſages of thoſe tragic poets, and were preſerved in the king's library at Paris.

The Memoirs of the Life of Racine are written by his ſon, who added to them ſome account of his father's friends, Boileau, Moliere, and la Fontaine.

" My father," ſays young Racine, " to difguſt
" my brother from writing verſes, and from
" fear that he ſhould attribute to my father's
" Tragedies the attention that was paid to
" him by the men of rank about the Court,
" ſaid to him, " Do not ſuppoſe that my verſes
" procure me all this notice. Corneille writes
" much finer verſes than I can do, yet no one
" pays him the leaſt attention. He is only
" admired in the mouths of the actors. So
" inſtead of tiring a company with reciting
" my own verſes (about which I never talk),
" I content myſelf with converſing with them
" in the way they like, and talking of things
" that amuſe them. My buſineſs with them
" is, to tell them how clever *they* are ; ſo that
" ſometimes when the Prince of Condé has
" paſſed many hours with me, you would be
" aſtoniſhed,

" astonished, were you present, to observe that I
" have not spoken five words; but by degrees I
" lead him on to talk, and he goes home much
" better pleased with himself than with me."

LE CLERC.

The candour and modesty of this great scholar were not less remarkable than his erudition. When his judgment was matured by age, he became ashamed of what he had written in his youth on the subject of Genesis. He made a public recantation of his error, by annexing afterwards to his Commentary on Genesis a Dissertation concerning Moses, the writer of that book of the Pentateuch, in which he acknowledged very fairly the errors he had given into in the first edition of his Commentary. " However," says the learned and pious Dr. Huntingford, " the censorious may be in-
" clined through malevolence to attribute a
" change of sentiments to improper motives,
" yet in the estimation of candid judges, ha-
" bituated to reflection, it sullies no man's
" honour to abandon a mistake and adopt a
" right principle. It degrades no man's un-
" derstanding to acknowledge that he has
" thought

"thought erroneously; but that after mature
"enquiry he has changed his opinion; for very
"little do they answer the purpose of increas-
"ing age, who become not ...... as
"they grow older. The Spanish proverb
"says, A wise man alters his opinion, but
"a fool never does; and Lord Chief
"Justice Mansfield often said, that to ac-
"knowledge that you were yesterday wrong,
"is but to let the world know that you are
"wiser to-day than you were yesterday."

MONTESQUIEU.

The posthumous Works of this writer were published in 1783. In a preface to an Oriental Tale, intitled 'Arsaces and Ismenia,' printed in them, he says, "He wrote that Tale "from a desire that he had to make even des- "potism agreeable to his countrymen; being "persuaded in his mind that a limited "monarchy (which, from the instability "of human affairs, was but too apt to dege- "nerate into despotism) was the government "best suited to the country of France.*"

---

* Through how many different changes of government have the French passed since they destroyed the regal one!

Of this opinion was the illustrious Thuanus, who thus concludes that master-piece of human composition, the Introduction to the History of his own Times: " O God, preserve
" his majesty the King (Henry the Fourth),
" and the Dauphin; for in their safety are in-
" cluded the peace, the concord, the security,
" and every thing that can be useful and salu-
" tary to France. Direct the councils of him
" (who has saved his country from ruin, and
" who now flourishes like a verdant tree near
" a gentle stream) to the promotion of peace,
" to the encouragement of good learning, and
" of all those arts that render a kingdom great
" and respectable. Permit good order, so
" agreeable to good minds, to bear the su-
" preme sway. May ancient faith and religion,
" ancient manners, the institutes of our an-

In the late skirmish for power amongst the members of the Directory, a few of the persons concerned in it had a plan to put the present Duke of Orleans upon the throne; so true is Machiavel's observation, " That those are much
" mistaken who think a republican government can con-
" tinue together long united."—" Nothing," says the Abbé de St. Pierre, " can be worse than a divided autho-
" rity; for if one party of those assembled in the govern-
" ment do not submit to the supreme authority, it becomes
" a scene of civil wars, and civil wars destroy a state. A
" republican government itself must be founded on this
" union of authority." *Rêves d'un Homme du Bien.*

" cestors,

"cestors, and the laws of the country, be
"restored. Disperse all new and monstrous
"opinions, all heresies in religion, the off-
"spring of ill-employed leisure. May there
"remain no schism in the house of God, but
"may peace of conscience and security in the
"state be confirmed. And, O eternal God
"of heaven (without whom we are nothing,
"and can do nothing)! I entreat and beseech
"thee to grant, through thy Holy Spirit, that
"in every thing I am now about to tell,
"liberty, faith, and truth may be established,
"no less with those who are living at present
"than with posterity; and that my work may
"be as free from any suspicion of flattery or
"of malice, as it is free from any suspicion
"of my undertaking it from motives of in-
"terest or lucre!"

Then follow some Alcaic Latin verses to Truth, of which the following lines are a feeble adumbration:

O TRUTH, who with the Gods hadst birth,
Hated, detested, scorn'd on earth!
Virtue's delight, and Vice's dread,
Whither, ah! whither art thou fled?

O, from thy native skies descend,
Thy course to wretched mortals bend;

With Modesty, of nothing vain,
And Innocence, without a stain;

Simplicity, in robes of white,
Candour, celestial virgin bright;
And man's sincerest, kindest friend,
Religion, on thy steps attend!

Then dare the dangers of the field,
Thy falchion draw, and grasp thy shield;
For oh! the latter days are near,
And ev'ry bosom shakes with fear.

The world, by age extreme decay'd,
By man's foul deeds a chaos made,
In ruin hurl'd, or wrapt in fire,
Shall in the vast abyss expire;

Unless thy salutary pow'r
Avert the dread tremendous hour;
Unless the magic of thy grace
Restore to virtue man's frail race.

To save the world then, Goddess! fly,
Destroy the fiend Impiety;
Rebellion's violence confound,
And licence, raging all around:

Concord's long wish'd for joys infuse,
And Peace, the nurse of ev'ry Muse;
Error's mad sophistry restrain,
And thy blest sway o'er men maintain:

' Gainst Vice's darts their bosoms steel;
Make them this precept's force to feel:
" Howe'er Affliction waves its rod,
" To follow thee, and fear their God."

M. DE SALO.

As this Counsellor of the Parliament of Paris was returning from the courts of justice one summer evening in the year 1662 (a year rendered memorable in the annals of France by a severe famine by which it was distinguished), followed only by his servant, a man came up and putting a pistol to his breast, whilst his hand trembled exceedingly, demanded his money. "My friend," said he, "you have "stopped an improper person; I have not "much money about me, but it is all at your "service;" and gave him two Louis. The man took them, and made off as fast as he could, without saying any thing more. "Fol- "low that man," said M. de Salo to his servant, "without his observing you; see "where he stops, and return and let me "know." The servant did as he was ordered, followed the robber through three or four narrow streets, and saw him go into a baker's shop, where he bought a large loaf of bread and changed one of his Louis. He then went into an alley at the distance of a few paces, ran up a pair of stairs that led to a garret, and on entering it (where there was no light but that of the moon) he threw his loaf

into

into the middle of the room, and exclaimed with sobs to his wife and children, "Eat, eat; "this loaf has cost very dear; satisfy your "hunger, and do not torment me as you have "done to procure you another. I shall be "hanged one of these days, and you will be "the cause of it." The wife, who was in tears, appeased him as well as she could, picked up the loaf, and divided it amongst her four children, who were nearly starved to death. The servant, who had taken exact notice of all that passed, returned to his master, who went the next morning according to his directions to visit the poor man's habitation. In his way up stairs he enquired of the lodgers what character he bore, and was told that he was a shoemaker, an honest and a worthy man, ever ready to assist his neighbours, but burdened with a large family; and so poor that they wondered how he was able to live. M. de Salo knocked at his door and was immediately let in by the poor man in rags, who, instantly recollecting him as the person that he had robbed the preceding day, fell down at his feet, requesting him not to ruin him. "Do not make yourself uneasy, my "good friend," said M. de Salo; "I am not "come to do you any harm I promise you. "You follow a very wretched profession I
"assure

" assure you, and one that will in a short
" time bring you to the gallows if you do
" not leave it off. Take these ten guineas,
" they will buy you some leather; so work
" as hard as you can, and support your chil-
" dren by your honest industry."

This incident gave rise to an affecting French drama called *L'Humanité*, and will, in the minds of persons of benevolence and charity, give rise to reflections that will end in something more real. It has been said, that many thousand persons died of hunger under the *ancien regime* of France. Mr. Saunders Welsh, an active and intelligent magistrate of Middlesex, told Dr. Johnson, he had good reason to think that in some years two thousand persons died of want in London *.
England

---

* A fastidious person was one day observing to Dr. Johnson how much she was affected by the smell of victuals in passing through Porridge Island, near St. Martin's church (a place filled with cooks' shops, that administer soup and meat to the necessitous and labouring poor of this metropolis), " Madam," said he, " let us have no sneering at what
" is so serious a thing to so many persons. Hundreds of
" your fellow-creatures turn another way that they may
" not be tempted by the luxuries of Porridge Island to wish
" for gratifications which they are not able to obtain. You
" are certainly not better than all of these; give God thanks
                                                " that

England may with great justice boast of its poor-laws; a system without rival in the world for its excellence and humanity, by which the rich are justly obliged to assist the suffering poor; and in which, perhaps, one alteration might be made with great propriety, that would render them as perfect as we can expect any thing to be that is done by man. The poor, who are honestly and worthily employed in another parish, should not in case of sickness be compelled to go to their own for assistance. A clause from the militia act might be easily adopted for this salutary and benevolent purpose *.

SUJA

" that you are happier." Noble and exalted sentiments like these have lately, in the midst of a dissipated and luxurious metropolis, given rise to an association which bears this honourable title, "*The Society for bettering the Condition* " *and increasing the Comforts of the Poor.*"

* The treasurer of the county in which the sick militia-man happens to be, is empowered to draw upon the treasurer of the county where the man's legal settlement is, for the expences that his illness has occasioned.———An excellent magistrate, in his charge to the overseers and churchwardens of the hundred of Stoke, Bucks, says wisely and humanely with respect to the removal of labourers belonging to other parishes, " Consider thoroughly what you may lose, and " what the individual may suffer by the removal, be-" fore you apply to the justices on the subject. When you
" have

SUJA AL DOULAH.

This energetic and active Indian Prince is thus described by the ingenious Mr. Dow:

"He is extremely handsome in his person, about five feet eleven inches in height, and so nervous and strong that with one stroke of a sabre he can cut off the head of a buffalo. He is active, passionate, and ambitious. His penetrating eye seems at first sight to promise uncommon acuteness and fire of mind; but his genius is too volatile for depth of thought, and he is consequently more fit for the manly exercises of the field than for deliberation in the closet. Till of late he gave little attention to business. He was up before the sun, mounted his horse, rushed into the forest, and hunted down tigers or deer till the noon of day; he then returned, plunged into the cold bath, and spent his afternoon in the Haram."

"have had for a long time the benefit of labour, and when all that is wanted is a little temporary relief, reflect whether, after so many years spent in your service, this is the moment and the cause for removing them from the scene of their labour to a distant parish."

KANG

KANG HI,

EMPEROR OF CHINA.

This great prince, in one of his excursions, observing a person sitting idle under a hedge, in a fit of rage, ordered one of his attendants to strip him of his clothes and make off with them. "A man," added he, "that does not work "himself, must always cause harm to some "other person." Solon, the wise legislator of Athens, commanded the Areopagus to watch over the conduct of every citizen, and to punish those that were idle. Dr. Huntingford says finely in one of his Discourses, "Whilst bodily strength is yet unimpaired by "debility, whilst our mental faculties are "neither embarrassed by necessity nor de"pressed by grief; during that happy period "of life to shrink from the labour either of "preparing for a creditable station, or of ably "filling it when undertaken; to shrink from "that labour for the sake of gratifying a "propensity to listless indolence, frivolous "trifling, or amusements then improper when "either unreasonable in point of time or in "their nature incompatible with our destina"tion: such conduct is cowardly and un"manly in the sight of reason; it is criminal "and culpable in the sight of Christianity;
"for

" for Christianity demands not only the avoid-
" ing of evil, but zealous activity in the per-
" formance of good works *."

The English proverb styles idleness ' The
' Devil's anvil ;' and some interpreters
have laboured to prove that the house in Scripture into which the bad spirits entered was
that of an idle man; and that its being swept
and garnished meant merely that it contained
nothing in it to occupy either the mind or the
body of its wretched possessor, but left them
to the complete occupancy and dominion of
any vice that was tempted by its vacuity to
take up its abode there. The pains and pe-
nalties of idleness were never more completely
exemplified than in the case of a linen-draper
of London who retired to his native country-
town to enjoy his leisure. He had not long
been from London before *ennui pleuvoit à
grosses goutes*, before he was harrassed with the
terrible disease of having nothing to do, and
became exceedingly low-spirited and despon-
dent. He was soon afterwards attacked with
the stone in a very severe manner; and when
his

* See Discourses in two volumes 8vo. by Dr. Huntingford, Warden of Winchester College. It should be recommended

his friends came to condole with him on his having so horrid and so painful a disorder, he said he was not certain but that the stone was a happy thing for him, as it gave him something to attend to and to think of. " Preserve me from myself, good God," is a Spanish wish; and it has been observed, that persons who have committed suicide, have been rather those who had nothing to do*, than those who were oppressed with business; rather those who had no sensations, than those who had painful ones. Sir William Davenant says finely in Gondibert,

> ————————toil does keep
> Obstructions from the mind and quench the blood;
> Ease but belongs to us like sleep, and sleep
> Like opium is our medicine, not our food.

The consequences of idleness are more mischievous and more to be dreaded in minds of a certain temper and vigour than in duller and feebler

mended to all parents and instructors of youth, to put into their hands these excellent Sermons, which combat the present dangerous opinions, and the prevailing vices of the times, with great force of argument, and with the most impressive energy of religious injunction.

* Dr. Hartley in his exquisite work, ' Observations on Man,' &c. recommends those persons who are hypochondriacal

feebler ones; as the weeds in a rich yet uncultivated soil are more in number and more rank and pernicious than in a field of less natural fertility.

GILES LE MAITRE,

first President of the Parliament of Paris in the reign of Henry the Second, inserted in all his leases with his farmers, a clause, that at the four great feasts of the year they should supply him with a covered cart, spread with fresh straw, to carry his wife and daughters, as well as with an ass to carry his chamber-maid: himself rode before them on a mule, and his clerk trotted by his side on foot. " The number of " livery servants," says St. Foix, " is a serious " evil at Paris. Those persons who were for- " merly contented with a maid servant, have " now two or three stout fellows as lacquies " behind their carriage. " I could wish," adds he, " that in time of war every second " servant were taken from behind the coach " and made to serve in the army. In one of " the Grecian republics, it was reckoned in- " famous in time of war for any citizen to " be attended in the streets by a servant."

derived from having nothing to do, to take up in a benevolent manner the concerns of others; to become interested about their welfare; and by sympathy to prevent the vacuum and the horrors of idleness.

MARSHAL SAXE.

This great commander said on his death-bed to his physician, "My dear Senac, life is a dream; I indeed have had a very splendid dream. Pray take care that my body be consumed by quicklime. I wish nothing to remain of me but my memory amongst my friends*."

The dissolution of the human body by these means would be productive of many advantages. It would prevent much occasion of contagion; the rites of sepulture would not be violated in the disgusting manner in which we have seen them in our times; and the awful sentence passed upon mankind, of "dust thou art, and to dust thou shalt return," would be as completely fulfilled as by the ordinary method of burial.

J. J. ROUSSEAU,

the legislator of the modern French, thus describes the government which they have

---

* Philip Verteyer, a celebrated anatomist of Louvain, desired to be buried in a field, and a stone with this inscription to be put over his grave:

"I, Philip Verteyer, have chosen this spot as my place of sepulture, from fear of profaning the sacred site of a church, and infecting the air of the city with unwholesome vapours."

chosen,

chosen, as they suppose upon his recommendation. " There is no government so subject
" to civil war and internal dissentions, as a
" democracy, or popular government. There
" is no one that tends so strongly, and so continually to change its form, nor that requires
" more vigilance and resolution to be maintained in it."

Habemus ergo confitentem reum!

A man too honest to disguise the mischiefs of the form of government which himself recommends.

GUSTAVUS ADOLPHUS,
KING OF SWEDEN.

This prince was of a very hasty disposition. He gave Colonel Seaton a slap on the face for something that he had done to displease him. Seaton demanded his dismission from the army, obtained it, and set off for the frontier of Denmark. The king, ashamed of the insult he had put upon a brave and an excellent officer, soon followed him on a fleet horse, and overtook him. " Seaton," said he, " I see
" you are offended, and I am the cause of
" it. I am sorry for it, as I have a very great
" regard for you. I have followed you hither
" to give you satisfaction. I am now, as you
" well

"well know, out of my own kingdom; so that at present Gustavus and Seaton are equals. Here are two pistols and two swords, avenge yourself if you please." Seaton immediately threw himself at the king's feet, and told him what ample satisfaction he had already given him for what he had done. They returned to Stockholm together, where Gustavus told this adventure to all his Court.

Marshal Gassion told Gustavus, "That the kings of France did not expose themselves so much in battle as he did."—"There is," replied the prince, "a great deal of difference between us; the kings of France are great monarchs, and I am only a soldier of fortune."

This prince, not long before he died, had his horse shot under him. An officer went to help him up, to whom he said coolly, "I have had a very narrow escape, the fruit, perhaps, is not quite ripe yet." He was killed at the battle of Lutzen. He had first his arm broke with a musket ball. A soldier saw it, and cried out, "The King is wounded."—"Say nothing about it, my friend," said the king; "it is nothing; follow me, and let us charge the enemy." Then turning towards the Prince of Saxe Lauenburgh, he said

said to him in a low tone of voice, "Cousin, "I believe I have enough of it. I am in very "great pain; pray try to get me off." At the same instant a ball passed through his body, and he fell down dead.

This great prince had then his with. He used to say, "That no men were so happy as those "who died in the exercise of their profession."

"Gustavus," says a French writer, "like "Scipio, was much addicted to study, and "found time to read a great deal in the midst "of his military operations. He used to say "in sport, that he was desirous to shew Gro- "tius the difference between theory and prac- "tice, and how easy it is to give political "precepts, and how difficult to put them in "execution."

~~~~~

PÈRE BUFFIER.

This learned jesuit wrote a Comedy in Latin iambics, called Democritus Rex; or, the Philosopher King. He exhibits the character of one of those *ci-devant* wise men, who are no less anxious to reform government than

every

every thing else. His sovereign takes him at his word, and resigns his crown to him, to enable him to carry his projects into execution. The new sovereign soon becomes bewildered in his unaccustomed dignity, and deviates from his own principles upon the first occasion. In short, matters turn out so ill under this reforming prince, unused to government, that he resigns the crown to its old possessor, and returns to his former situation.

PIETRO PAOLO SARPI

appears to have been one of the greatest characters that history has consecrated to the memory of mankind. As an historian, he is, perhaps, take him altogether, one of the purest and most dignified that ever wrote. No unnecessary digressions, no useless and affected observations sully the simplicity and correctness of his narration. He proceeds in it, like a temperately-flowing river, neither deluging its banks, nor impeded by any obstacle to its course. His defence of the liberties of his country against the attacks of the see of Rome, will ever entitle him to the kindest remembrance of the manly yet candid patriot. His

knowledge

knowledge was various and extensive. He was no less a good chemist and excellent anatomist, than he was a profound divine. His morals were those which even inspired a cloyster with superior piety; and his courage would have done honour to the most intrepid General.

He was buried in the convent of the Servites (that of his own order) at Venice, his funeral being attended by the Doge, and the principal senators of the republic. His monument was thus inscribed:

AULUS VENETUS SERVITARUM ORDINIS THEOLOGUS,

Ita prudens, ita sapiens, ut majorem nec humanorum, nec divinorum scientiam,

Nec integriorem, nec sanctiorem vitam desiderares.

Intelligentiâ per cuncta, permanente sapientiâ et affectus dominante præditus,

Nullâ unquam cupiditate commotus, nullâ animi ægritudine turbatus.

Semper constans, moderatus, perfectus, verum innocentiæ exemplar:

Deo mirâ pietate, religione, continentiâ addictus:

Reipublicæ, in sui desiderium concitatæ, justam, fidelem operam navans:

(Religiosum hominem, dum patriæ servit, haud à Deo separare existimans)

Summâ consilii, rationis vi, liberâ, integrâ mente, publicam causam defendens:

Magnas à Libertate Venetâ insidias sapientiâ suâ repellens:

Majus

Majus libertatis præsidium in se, quam in Arcibus positum, Venetis ostendens :
Mortales, an magis amandus, mirandus, venerandus, dubios faciens :
De Nominis apud probos æternitate, de animi apud Deum immortalitate securus,
Morbum negligens, mortem contemnens, loquens, docens, orans, contemplans
Vivorum actiones exercens,
LXXI Æt.
Magno Bonorum Ploratu,
Non obiit ;
Abiit è vitâ, ad vitam evolavit.
Jo. Antonius Venerius Patricius Venetus
Mærens posuit.
Anno. Sal. M. DC. XXIII.

Father Paul, in his last illness, occasioned by a wound* from a stiletto directed by the

* On receiving this wound, at a time in which he was writing against the papal usurpations, he exclaimed " *Conosco lo stylo Romano.* " I heard the King James the' " First saye, that of late in Venice there was a practice of " a priest discovered, which was to blowe up by a trayne " of powder Pietro Paolo, his books and him; but that it " was discovered by a stranger passenger, that took excep- " tions to see a lyght in a vault at that tyme of night." *MS. letter of the time.* Father Paul was well affected to the Protestant religion, and particularly to that form of it professed by the Church of England; but when exhorted to profess it openly, he said, " That it was better for himself, " like St. Paul, to be anathema for his brethren; and that " he did more service to the Protestant religion by wearing " that habit, than he could do by lying it aside."

court

court of Rome, received the visit of the doge and senate of Venice in bed. He had just strength enough to raise himself up on their entrance, and with his hands closed, and his eyes lifted towards heaven, exclaimed, " *Esto* " *perpetua:* May the liberties of my country " last for ever!" A wish to be repeated by every Englishman, who deserves the blessings which his country affords him. Father Paul's wish gave rise to the concluding lines of the following Prologue, which was spoken in the autumn of 1797, at that excellent seminary of learning, of virtue, and of religion, the school of the Rev. Dr. Valpy, at Reading.

PROLOGUE
TO THE
AMPHITRYO OF PLAUTUS,
PERFORMED AT READING SCHOOL FOR THE BENEFIT OF THE PHILANTHROPIC SO-
CIETY.

YOU, who so oft this favour'd spot have grac'd,
The kind, indulgent arbiters of taste,
Once more our scenic labours now attend,
Once more our well-intended mirth befriend.
What happier omens can our efforts greet?
Affection, beauty, learning, candour meet.

This night we tell a tale from days of yore,
Deck'd in each elegance of classic lore.
We tell from Plautus how the mighty Jove
(Such is the magic pow'r of mightier Love)

Left

Left his celestial realms to visit earth,
And to Alcmena's valiant son gave birth,
To Hercules, through Time's long records known,
" The injur'd world's avenger, and his own."
Nor least this toil; the Hydra fell he slew,
Who from each wound increasing vigour drew;
And as the Hero each dire head suppress'd,
Another head uprear'd its hissing crest.

O grant, kind Heav'n, in these degen'rate times,
With vices satiate, and profuse of crimes;
Whilst with Impiety's dread flag unfurl'd,
A thousand mental monsters range the world;
Whilst luxury its baleful charms retails,
And ev'ry age, and rank, and sex assails;
See hosts of vot'ries the contagion gain,
Whilst reason, prudence, justice, plead in vain;
See how they tempt the utmost verge of fate,
Till sad experience teaches but too late;
Till ruin's ruthless fangs the victims seize,
And to each mis'ry doom the sons of ease:
See the curst die each social feeling blast,
Set fortune, health, and honour on a cast;
Like the fam'd Pontiff's rod, of sov'reign pow'r,
Each other passion with fell throat devour;
By fury urg'd, the yawning gulph despise,
Nor heed or duty's calls or nature's cries.
Whilst love its sacred empire now disdains,
And links no more two minds in mutual chains:
For our convenience now alone we wed,
Soon mutual falsehood stains the nuptial bed;
And the adult'rer, mark'd with no disgrace,
Keeps in life's intercourse his wonted place:
Whilst Suicide, the offspring of despair,
With pallid cheeks, and eyes of lurid glare,

When

When dangers threaten, and misfortunes low'r,
Dares to usurp th' Eternal Master's pow'r,
And, with a coward's impotence of soul,
Points the sharp steel, or drains the envenom'd bowl,
And, to avoid a moment's fleeting pain,
Consigns itself to Torment's endless reign.—
O grant, kind Heav'n, a moral Hercules,
To bid these horrors from the land to cease;
With giant arm avert the foul disgrace,
And vindicate the honours of our race.

Arise, thou sacred Genius of the isle,
And, as of old, on thy lov'd country smile;
And O protect with thy benignant wing
Her youthful sons, her hope, her pride, her Spring*;
May no rank weeds of pestilential pow'rs
Destroy the sweetness of their op'ning flow'rs!
May in their hearts no baleful ivy shoot,
And blast the promise of the fairest fruit;
Their dawn of reason no false glare infest,
But Truth's bright Ægis sparkle on their breast;
Their souls' soft pow'rs no blandishments ensnare,
And no fell passions their young bosoms tear;
But useful learning, by true taste refin'd,
Increase the native vigour of the mind!
Their innate purity may labour guard,
And honest fame bestow its earn'd reward;
Religion's panoply their virtues shield,
Then " more than conqu'rors" in life's arduous field.

* Pericles, having in one of his Orations occasion to lament the death of many of the young men at Athens slain in battle, says beautifully, " The year has lost its Spring," the season of promise and of expectation; the season of those blossoms that prognosticate the finest fruit.

Each

Each noble deed their country's love inspire,
And join the hero's to the patriot's fire;
And in her laws revere the noblest plan
That man's best wisdom form'd for ruling man;
Where mutual ties the peer and peasant bind;
And Princes govern but to bless mankind;
Where scale of rank but fans the mind's bright flame,
And bids it by desert at honours aim;
Bids Virtue, by no preference opprest,
To equal glory rear her manly crest,
Which, like the pyramid, Time's wreck defies,
Nor fears or driving storms, or angry skies.
Where freedom, by gradation stronger grown,
Offers its grateful homage to the Throne;
Which, as the point, bestows the higher grace,
Whilst the blest people form the solid base.

 Then fear not, Britons, though the sons of France
Their legions to this happy land advance;
Though, flush'd with conquest in their mad career,
Their course through envy to this isle they steer;
Sure that, in mercy to a suff'ring world,
Heav'n's vengeance on its scourges will be hurl'd;
And boldly hope that Holland's recent fate
The rash invader's efforts shall await;
To DUNCAN, HOWE, and JERVIS, safely trust,
Whilst British valour proves the skies still just.
Then with the dying Paolo exclaim,
Whilst his last accents bless'd Venetia's name,
" No foreign foe my country's safety blast,
" And may its liberties for ever last *!"   S.

* Many persons have wondered at the attachment of this excellent and liberal-minded man to the government of his country, which was most assuredly inimical to general liberty.

BEAUMELLE.

With what triumph must an Englishman hear this acute Frenchman say, "The English
" pass in the world for understanding matters
" of finance better than any other people in
" Europe. It is their Constitution that under-
" stands for them. The solidity of the Eng-
" lish credit makes that nation draw immense
" wealth from a method of borrowing that
" would destroy a private person. In France
" (he speaks of the *ancien regime*) a loan
" creates a debt, and often a want. In Eng-
" land, a loan extinguishes a want and at the
" same time creates a revenue *.

b..ty. He most probably consid red in affairs of government how difficult a matter it was to arrive at perfection;
of that of a revolution the immediate ill consequences were
       and certain, the event completely enveloped in the
womb of time, and not worth putting into risk and hazard
the pre sent advantages which it afforded. "Woe, said he,"
says Clermont Galeerellot, " to all persons who are so un-
" happy as to live in the time of a revolution!"

* The Patriots of ancient Greece and Rome gained their
renown by loving their country, and exalting its advantages.
In our time, those who wish to bear that honourable title
       to it by affecting to hate theirs, and to depreciate its
              as if they had received their lessons from the Di-
            of the French Rep blic.
                                          " England

" England is a striking proof, that a Constitution which nothing can affect is a blessing that can never be bought too dear.

" The Constitution of England must be immortal; for a wise people can never be enslaved by an enemy from without; nor can a free people ever be enslaved by an enemy from within *.

" Rome has perished, and could not have subsisted. Its system tended to its greatness, and not to its preservation. England is arrived at that point at which it can never perish; for its revolutions, which should have been the destruction of its system, have been the corroboration of it †."—*Mes Pensées, 12mo, Amsterdam, 1752.*

---

* " The Constitution of England," says a man of images one day, " is like a compass set upon jumbles, the needle of which, whatever concussions it may have, always turns to the true point; the point on which the real happiness and safety of the country depend."

† The great Duke of Rohan says, " England is an enormous animal, which can never die except by suicide; unless it kills itself."—*Interests des Etats.*

PETER-

PETER THE GREAT,

CZAR OF RUSSIA.

On seeing the mausoleum of Cardinal Richlieu at Paris, Peter exclaimed, " There lies a " man to whom I would have given half my " dominions if he would have taught me to " have governed the other half."

He was not appalled by the extraordinary successes of Charles XII. " I know very " well," said he, " that the Swedes will beat " us; but at last they themselves will teach us " to beat them."

When he sent his propositions for peace to Charles, that Prince haughtily replied, " I " will treat with Peter in the capital of his " dominions only." When this answer was brought to Peter he said coolly, " My brother " Charles is continually affecting to act the " part of Alexander; but I flatter myself that " he will not find in me a Darius."

His strength of mind increased under danger and difficulty. When he saw his army give way before Leuenhaupt, he ran to the rear guard of it, and exclaimed to the Cossacs and " Calmucs,

Calmucs, " I order you to fire directly upon " any one who shall not keep his post, and " even to fire upon me the first of all if I " should be coward enough to attempt to " fly." This intrepid behaviour decided the fate of Charles at Pultowa's calamitous day.

When the battle was over, he invited the principal Swedish officers to dine with him in his tent; and after dinner rising gravely from his seat he drank the health of his masters in the art of war. One of the Swedish generals said, " Pray, Sir, to whom does your Majesty " give that very honourable title?"—" To " you, gentlemen," replied the Czar.—" Then " your Majesty has just treated your masters " with great ingratitude," said another of the Swedish officers.—" I will repair that," said the Czar, " as well as I can," and immediately ordered their swords to be returned to them, and treated them with great politeness and attention all the time they continued his prisoners.

In his projects of reform, Peter made great use of M. Le Fort, a Genevese captain of artillery, whom he had met with by chance, and with whom his soul immediately accorded by congeniality of talents.

The

The upper part of the Czar's face was handsome; the lower part, particularly the mouth, was apt to be convulsed by a natural defect, which was but too much increased by the violence of his temper, and by those impetuous *

* In those transports of anger no one ventured to approach him except his Empress, the beauteous and the gentle Catherine. He would occasionally sit down at her feet while he was in those paroxysms of fury, and suffer her to press his throbbing temples with her soft and delicate hands, while the accents of her voice, "like the sweet "south," composed and harmonized his mind, and he rose up restored to the dignity of his nature and the proper exertion of his talents. What a subject for a picture! It appears astonishing that no artist has ever attempted to delineate this interesting and affecting scene.

Rowlie, or Chatterton (it matters not who when he writes so beautifully), says in the interlude of 'Ella,'

    Angells be wroghte to bee of neidher kynde,
      Angells alleyne fromme chafe desire be free;
    Dheere is a somewhat evere yn in the mind
      Yatt without woman cannot styiled bee;
No seyncte in celles, botte having blodde and tere
Do synde the spright to joie on syghte of womanne fayre.

    Albeyte withouten wommen, menne were pheers
      To salvage kynd and wulde botte live to slea;
    Botte womanne eft the spryghte of peace, so cheers
      Tochelod yn angel joie heie angels bee.

transports of anger by which he suffered himself to be too often agitated.

Peter in his infancy had a dread of the water. This antipathy he corrected by dint of perseverance; and half his time was spent in exertions of mind upon that very element, the mere sight of which when he was a child used to throw him into fits.

Voltaire's history of this Prince is very defective and superficial. He somewhere calls him, "*moitié heros, moitié tygre,*" a compound of the hero and the tiger; a compound perhaps highly necessary to subjugate the minds and reform the manners of his subjects; who, when he came to reign over them, were in a very barbarous and ferocious state.

The following is an extract of a Letter from the learned Mr. Wanley to Dr. Charlett:

"The Czar gave the king's (King Wil-
"liam) servants at his departure one hun-
"dred and twenty guineas, which was
"more than they deserved, they being very
"rude to him; but to the King he pre-
"sented a rough ruby, which the greatest
"jewellers of Amsterdam (as well Jews as
"Christians)

" Christians) valued at 10,000l sterling. It
" is bored through; and when it is cut and
" polished it must be set upon the top of the
" imperial crown of England.

" I cannot vouch for the following bill of
" fare, which the Czar and his company
" (thirteen at table in all) eat up at Godal-
" min in Surry; but it is averred for truth
" by an eye-witness who saw them eating,
" and had this bill from the landlord:—At
" breakfast, half a sheep, one quarter of lamb,
" ten pullets, one dozen of chickens, three
" quarts of brandy, six quarts of mulled wine,
" seven dozen of eggs, with sallads in pro-
" portion: At dinner, five ribs of beef three
" stone weight, one sheep fifty pounds
" weight, three quarters of a lamb, a shoulder
" and loin of veal boiled, eight pullets, four
" couple of rabbits, two dozen and a half of
" sack, and one dozen of claret."

The Czar soon after his voyage to England
visited France, and was received with great
politeness by the Regent. He seemed much
pleased with the country and the people; and
on quitting them appeared to observe with
great regret, that by their luxury they were
hastening on to their destruction.

" This

"This prince," says the good Abbé de St. Pierre, "owed his extreme application to the business of government to the conspiracy that was formed against him in 1690. As he was not willing to run the same risque again, he found that application to business would render him in a short time more intelligent, more respected by his subjects, and better served by his ministers. The Czar had a great desire to have a port in the Baltic sea; so by means of his ambassador he proposed to the King of Sweden to yield him up Narva, or some port in that sea, in exchange for some other territory of his own, or for a sum of money; but he was not prudent enough to offer either a territory or a sum of money equivalent to the value of this port; so that the King of Sweden might be tempted to sell him upon advantageous terms to himself what was of little value to him. He was likewise imprudent in another respect; his ambassador had orders to take by force what the King refused to sell or to exchange; and this menace indisposed the King, who was as violent and as bold as himself, against him. The Czar, too, might have been sure that a war of two years only would have cost him four times as much as any sale or voluntary

"exchange

" exchange could have done; and, besides,
" he was not certain of being victorious in
" the war. Observe, then, how dearly it
" costs ill-advised and imprudent princes
" when they make use of disgusting menaces
" in negociations, where the point in dispute
" should be settled on a consideration of their
" reciprocal interests.

" It is true," continues this honest politician, " that it must have been a great pleasure
" to the Czar to have travelled incognito and
" at his ease in England and in Holland, and
" to have seen their different dock-yards,
" vessels, troops, &c. It was the pleasure of
" a young man who loves to see a variety of
" objects. These pleasures may be allowed to
" rich private persons, who at a certain
" age, for want of accustoming themselves to
" read and to think, have nothing better to do,
" or at least will do nothing better; but in a
" prince who has every day something to do,
" and subjects to govern, it is a pleasure out
" of its place. But what makes all this the
" less allowable is, that the Czar undertook
" these travels at a time when the conspiracy
" was not entirely at an end, and when the
" punishments in consequence of it merely
" served to make persons more discontented
" and

" and difaffected to government. So after he
" had been abfent fifteen months, and was
" going to fet out for Italy, he was obliged
" to return to Ruffia on account of the break-
" ing out of a new confpiracy; and, after all,
" the only advantage that he drew from his
" travels was to have occafioned a great
" number of workmen of all kinds, of fhip-
" builders, and of land and fea officers, to
" come and fettle in Ruffia. But all thefe
" he might have obtained by other and lefs
" dangerous and expenfive methods, by means
" of his ambaffadors at the different courts,
" who might have engaged them by promifes
" and by money to come and fettle in his
" dominions; and he would not have been
" continually rifking his life in his difguife as
" a fhip-builder or failor, in which he might
" have been affaffinated any night at Sardam."
Rêves d'un homme de bien.

CATHERINE THE SECOND,

EMPRESS OF RUSSIA.

THIS great Princefs had the following fentence frequently in her mouth, "it is better to do
" amifs than to be continually changing one's
" opinion.

" opinion. Nothing is so contemptible as
" irresolution." This power of decision of
mind enabled Catherine to add so many
dominions to her own, and to give laws to
them *.

What excellent order this Empress preserved in her finances appears by the following letter to Voltaire, who was afraid that his tenants had sent her too many of the watches of their fabrication at Ferney:

" Do not scold your good folks for having
" sent me too many of their watches. The
" cost of them will not ruin me. I should
" be a very wretched being indeed if my fi-
" nances were so far reduced that I could not

---

* " After all," says she in one of her letters to Voltaire,
" those laws about which there is so much talk are not yet
" made. It is posterity and not ourselves that must judge
" on the question. I beg you to consider that they are to
" serve for Europe and for Asia. What a difference of
" climate, of persons, of customs, and even of ideas! Behold
" me now in Asia. I wished to see all this with my own eyes.
" There are in this city (Casan) twenty different nations,
" not in the least alike. I must, however, make a dress
" that will suit them all. Some general principles for
" them all may be found; but the details! and what de-
" tails!——I was going to say it is a whole world to
" create, to unite, and to preserve!"

" have

" have upon certain emergencies such small
" sums as will pay for these watches. Judge
" not, I beseech you, of our finances by those
" of the ruined sovereigns of Europe. Though
" we have now been engaged in a war for
" three years, we proceed with our buildings,
" and every thing else goes on as in time of
" profound peace. We buy pictures*. It is
" two years since any new tax has been raised.
" The present war has its fixed expence; that
" once regulated, it never disturbs the course
" of other affairs."

Catherine was in religious matters a pupil of Voltaire and the pretended French philosophers,

Cultrix Deorum Parca et infrequens;

yet soon after the massacre of the good Louis XVI. she went in solemn procession with her feet naked and her eyes uplifted to the monastery of St. Alexander Newsky. She perceived but too late the connection between religion and good government, and that those

---

* The Houghton collection, which was suffered to be sent out of England for less than thirty-six thousand pounds. Not the expence of one day of the present war.—*Credite, posteri!*

who fear God are not deficient in honouring the King. "If the infatuation of princes," says the pious and sagacious Dr. Hartley, "were not of the deepest kind, they could not but see that they hold their dominions *entirely* by the real Christianity that is left among us; and that if they succeed in taking away this foundation, or weakening it much farther, their governments must fall like houses built upon sand*. Besides the great influence which Christianity has to make man humble and obedient, it is to be considered that our ancestors have so interwoven it with the constitutions of the kingdoms of Europe, that they must stand or fall together. Christianity is the *cement* † of the building."

* This has so lately taken place in France, that we must be blind indeed not to have noticed it, and we may truly apply to Britain from Horace,

———tua res agitur; paries cum proximus ardet;

and from the fatal history of that country we may learn how little efficacious the principles of patriotism and of honour alone, without the aid of religion, are in correcting the most detestable vices and the most enormous crimes.

† "The English having attained a light in religion," says Selden, whom no one can suspect of bigotry, "that will own their liberties, of them both they made up *one* garland, not to be tricked by any rude hand."—*Selden's Discourses on Government.*

See 'Observations on Man, his Frame, his
'Duty, and his Expectations.' By David
Hartley, M. A. 2 vols. 8vo.

CHARLES XII.
KING OF SWEDEN.

MARSHAL SCHWERIN, who had served
under Charles, gave Voltaire the following
account of this intrepid warrior's method of
attacking the enemy. He called his officers
together when he intended to give battle, and
after having given them his orders respecting the
disposition of his army and other details, he was
impatient till they were complied with, and
was continually urging dispatch. These being
effected, he mounted his horse, put himself
at the head of his troops; drew his sword
with great ardour; and, striking with it right
and left without any discrimination, rushed
into the midst of the enemy.

Charles was pressed by Count Piper, after
he had completely defeated Augustus, King
of Poland, to take possession of that kingdom
for himself. He sternly refused, and gave it
to Stanislaus, repeating, " It is much more
" noble

"noble to give away kingdoms, than to ac-
"quire them."

Arithmetical enquiries* were favourite pursuits of his. He used to call a man ignorant
of

* The knowledge of arithmetic is not sufficiently cultivated at our great schools. The first Lord Lyttleton,
a nobleman of great learning and eloquence, when he became Chancellor of the Exchequer, was so ignorant of
arithmetic, that the sums of money, for which he had to
apply to the House of Commons, were put down for him
in letters, not in numbers. Osborn, in his celebrated Advice
to a Son, says, " Fathers, especially rich ones, are so far to
" learn themselves what is most fit that their children
" should be taught, as they keep them so long in their
" Latin school till the time is lapsed most proper for read-
" ing and to make a perfect *accomptant*, the most necessary
" part of mathematics, and so much as cannot be in any
" commerce spared. It remaining indubitable that none
" so industrious as to call himself to a weekly or at least
" an annual reckoning did ever through his own default
" spend an estate; whereas the want of this first rudiment
" of thrift hath within the compass of my experience
" brought divers to a bit of bread, and demolished the
" houses of the most eminent gentry of England.

" Now if any desire to understand how our more *illiterate*
" fathers came to escape this curse, an answer lies ready,
" that the greatest part of their revenues did consist in pro-
" visions of all sorts, paid punctually at a day, and so easily
" accounted for and remembered. And this abundance
" they

of arithmetic a half man; and, according to Voltaire, he wished to change the common method of numeration.

~~~~~

HENRY THE SECOND,
DUKE OF GUISE.

"Nothing," says Charron, " is so incon-
" stant, so fluctuating, and so timorous as
" the mob. The least opposition disconcerts
" them, and their leaders are in general the
" first to desert them and leave them a prey

" they enjoyed kept them pleased and in friendship with
" their estates, wanting neither company nor respect;
" through which they became less liquorish after the glory
" and small delights of London and of the court, towards
" which they did seldom look but upon constraint, having
" never tasted them (as they now do) in youth, *the only
" time to contract an affection to any place or thing.*"

" Nothing amuses more harmlessly than computation," says Dr. Johnson, with his usual strength of observation;
" and nothing is more often applicable to real business or
" speculative enquiries. A thousand stories which the ig-
" norant hear and believe die away when the computist
" takes them within his gripe. Numerical enquiries give
" entertainment in solitude by the practice, and reputation
" in public by the effect."

" to

"to their fears and imaginations. The Duke
"of Guise was one day roughly treated by
"the mob of Naples, by whom he had been
"sent for to govern them. He was mounted
"on an Arabian courser, with which he trod
"two or three of them under foot. One of
his friends remonstrated with him on the occasion. He replied with all the *fierté* of his ancient and illustrious house, ' When the Deity
"creates a man of my rank, he always puts
"something between his eyes which a black-
"guard dare not look at."

In our times Cardinal Maury and the Lord Chancellor of Ireland have seen what wonderful effects personal courage and presence of mind have had upon the multitude.

~~~~~

MAURICE,
PRINCE OF ORANGE.

At the celebrated siege of Breda the army of this Prince was seized with the scurvy, and became torpid and enervated. The Prince caused letters to be sent into the town assuring the garrison of immediate relief from a large army that was on their march,

and

and accompanied the letters with a few small phials of a supposed remedy against the scurvy, so efficacious that a few drops only, mixed with a gallon of water, would prove a specific against the disease. The physicians were in the secret, and administered the remedy with great pomp of manner and affectation of caution. The garrison were cured, and recovered their strength and spirits; and the 'Princes Drops' became afterwards a *nom de guerre* in the Low Countries.

BARILLON,

ambassador from France to Charles the Second and James the Second, is thus described by Madame de Sevigné:

"*Il est riche, gros, et vieux; il n'est pas gaté d'ambassade de dix ans.*

Son emploi est admirable* cette année 1673.

Il mangera cinquante mille francs cette année, mais il sçait bien où les prendre.

* The French have been ever remarkable for managing their political concerns with other nations by giving or taking money. See Barillon's Dispatches, and the recent Declarations of the American Ministers at Paris.

JOHN DE WITT.

Some one asked this great statesman how he could go through so much business. "By doing one thing * at a time," replied he.

One of his maxims was, that a man should be careful of his health and careless of his life; careful of that glorious boon of Heaven without which nothing effectual is to be done; and careless of that gift of heaven which is bestowed upon us merely as a loan to be sacrificed to duty, to honour, and to principle, and which is ill redeemed at the expence of either.

*Summum crede nefas animum preferre pudori
Et propter vitam vivendi perdere causas.*

De Witt seems to have too good an opinion of the wisdom of the congregated part of mankind when he says, that a state will always

---

* The late Duke of Newcastle, secretary of state, &c. appeared always in a hurry in business. It was said of him, "that he had lost one hour in the morning, which he was "looking for the whole day afterwards." Of a person in a hurry Lord Chesterfield says well, "that he plainly shews "his business is too much for him."

pursue

pursue its own interest. Good sense, courage, and simplicity, were the characteristics of his mind. With what intrepidity he bore the outrages of the multitude is well known. A traveller tells with what admiration he saw De Witt, who had put his name to treaties by the side of those of emperors and of kings, walk accompanied with one servant only behind him to the Council House of the Hague.

To this great man England is indebted for the talents of one of its distinguished princes, William the Third, whose education De Witt superintended with extreme attention, and by severe and exact discipline taught him the art of reigning.

ELIZABETH,

QUEEN OF ENGLAND.

Previous to the attack of the Spanish Armada this magnanimous Princess composed the following Prayer, which she ordered to be used daily in every ship of the British navy:

" Most Omnipotent Maker and giver of all
" the world's mass, that only searchest and
" fathomest

" fathomest the bottom of all hearts and con-
" ceits, and in them seest the true original of
" all actions intended; thou that by thy fore-
" sight dost truly discern how no malice of
" revenge, nor quittance of injuries, nor desire
" of bloodshed, nor greediness of lucre, had
" moved the resolution of our new set-out
" army; but a needful care and very watch
" that no neglect of foes or over surety of
" promise might breed either danger in us or
" glory in them. These being the grounds
" (thou that dost inspire the mind) we humbly
" beseech thee with bended knees prosper the
" work, and with the best forewinds guide
" the journey, speed the victory, and make
" the return the advancement of thy glory,
" the triumph of their fame, and safety of the
" realm with the least loss of English blood.
" To these alone petitions Lord give thou thy
" blessed grant. Amen."

Duplessis Mornay says in his Notes in the third volume of the History of Thuanus,

" The Prince of Orange always called me
" an infidel, because I had always said from
" what I knew of Queen Elizabeth, that she
" had never any serious thoughts of marriage.
" The prince sent for me soon afterwards, and
" told

"told me, that he had received a letter from
"M. de Sainte Aldegonde, the Duke d'Alen-
"con's agent in England, which informed
"him, that when the contract for his master's
"marriage with Queen Elizabeth was pre-
"sented to her to sign at the council table,
"she threw it on the ground trembling with
"anger, and turning herself towards the pri-
"vy councillors she exclaimed, Wretches that
"you are, are you so blind as not to see that
"after my death you will go to cutting each
"other's throats; and do you not know that
"if I am married I shall not live long after-
"wards? The latter part of this sentence,
"adds he, was supposed to regard some
"natural defect which she had, very little
"known."

In one of the Letters published in the exquisite Collection made by Mr. Lodge, that of Michael Brakingbury to Lord Talbot, it is said,

"Theyse sportts were great, and done in
"costly sort, to her Majesty's great lykinge and
"theyr great cost. To express every part
"with sundry devyses, yt ys more fytt for theme
"that delyteth in theme thane for me who
"estemeth lyttel suche vanyties I thanke God.
                                    "Thene

"Thenc the 19th day, *beynge Saynt Eliza-
"beth's da.*, the Erle of Comerland, the Erle
"of Essexe, and my L. Burge dyd chaleng
"all comers, six courses apeace, whiche was
"very honourablye performed."

In

* "The observation of this day as a Court festival,"
adds the ingenious Selector, " seems to have been one of
" those absurd pieces of flattery which was so common in
" this reign; and, perhaps, is no where mentioned but in
" the letter before us. Elizabeth was so insignificant a
" saint as to have no particular service allotted to her in the
" ancient rituals, except a short solitary lesson on the 19th
" of November; and the reformed breviary of Pius V. de-
" prives her even of that, and denies her a place in its Ca-
" lendar. The miracle to which this lady owed her canoni-
" zation was this: A comely young man, too gaily habited,
" coming to visit her, Elizabeth admonished him to deteste
" the vanities of the world. The young man answered,
" Madam, I beseech you pray for me."—" If thou wouldst
" have me pray for thee," said Elizabeth, " go thou and
" do likewise." So they began to pray at some distance,
" till the young man, unable to endure the fervour of her
" devotion, began to cry aloud, " that he should be de-
" stroyed by it;" whereupon her maidens running up to
" him found him all on fire, so that they could not touch
" his clothes, but were fain hastily to withdraw their hands,
" with such a vehement heat did he burn. Elizabeth here-
" upon ceased to pray; and the young man, inspired by
" this divine warmth, went into the order of the Francis-
" cans." *Reflections upon the Devotion of the R. C.
Church, London,* 1674. " Our Queen, who resembled
" the saint only in her name, and in her fondness for prac-

" tising

In a letter of John Stanhope to Lord Talbot, in the same Collection, it is said, "Thys night, God wylling, she (Queen Elizabeth) wyll go to Rychmond, and on Saturday next to Somersett house, and yf she could overcum her passyon against my Lo. of Essex for his maryadge no doubt she would be much the quyeter; yett doth she use ytt more temperately than was thought for, and (God be thanked) doth not strike all she thretes."

"tising on the weakness of comely young men, was silly enough to connive at the public recollection of this wretched legend, for the sake of the wretched compliment which the courtiers had founded on it." *Illustrations of British History, Biography, Manners, &c. by Edward Lodge, Esq. Vol. III.* a Work which cannot be too highly praised, when we consider the extreme curiosity of the ancient letters that the diligent Editor has drawn from hidden sources; or the excellent remarks and observations with which they are accompanied; or the characters of the persons which introduce the letters. The characters seem pourtrayed by Titian himself, so naturally and so accurately are they drawn, and display so intimate an acquaintance with history and human nature. Mr. Lodge's Books most assuredly deserve a place in the library of every lover of English history and English literature."

LORD BURLEIGH

laid down thefe maxims for managing fuits at Council table:

" Never to fuffer the lawyers to wrangle or
" digreffe in pleading.

" Counfellors are to deal truly and plainly
" with clients, and if their matter be naught
" to tell them fo, and not to footh them.

" When a poor man brings his council to
" the bar, and the other party fails, ever to
" award the poor man his cofts."

" Lord Burleigh commended the ftudie of
" the common law above all other," fays his
biographer; " and faid that if he were to begin
" his life again, he would follow that ftudie *."

EARL OF ESSEX.

WHEN this accomplifhed nobleman was in Ireland, and the rebellious Tyrone talked to him

* " Law," faid Dr. Johnfon one day very finely, " is the
" laft refult of human wifdom acting upon human expe-
" rience for the benefit of mankind."

of a toleration of religion, he replied, "Hang thee up, thou carest for religion as much as my horse." When he was solicited by his friends to bring his great personal enemy, Sir Walter Raleigh, to a court marial for some military misbehaviour in the island of Madeira, he coolly replied, "Sir, I would were he my friend."

Lord Essex was the most accomplished nobleman this country ever produced. He was polished in his manners, had a fine person, was extremely humane and generous, an excellent man of business, learned himself, and an encourager of learning in others, and an excellent writer in prose and verse. He drew up some directions for travellers, for the use of his nephew the Earl of Rutland, which are only to be found in a little volume now become very scarce. They are reprinted in this COLLECTION, together with some directions on the same subject by Sir Philip Sydney.

The late E. of E. his Advice to the E. of R. in his Trauels.

"My Lord,

"I hold it for a principle in the course of
"intelligence of state, not to discourage men
"of

"of meane capacity from writing vnto mee;
"though I had at that same time very able
"advertisements, for either they sent mee
"matter which the other omitted, or made it
"clearer by describing the circumstances; or,
"if added nothing, yet they confirmed that
"which coming single I might have doubted.
"This rule I have, therefore, prescribed to
"others, and now give it unto myselfe, yet
"doth my love direct these few lines to the
"study of you. If you find out nothing but
"that which you have from others, yet, per-
"haps, by the opinion of others, I confirme
"the opinion of wiser than myselfe. Your
"Lordship's purpose is to travel, and your
"study must bee what vse to make thereof.
"The question is ordinary, and there is to it
"an ordinary answer; that is, your Lordship
"shall see the beauties of many cities, know
"the manners of the people of many coun-
"tries, and learne the language of many na-
"tions. Some of these may serve for orna-
"ments, al of them for delight. But your
"Lordship must looke further than these
"things, for the greatest ornament is the
"beauty of the minde; and when you have
"as great delight as the world can afford you,
"you will confesse that the greatest delight is
"*sentire te indies fieri meliorem*. Therefore your
"Lordship's

"Lordship's end and scope should be, that
"which in moral philosophy we call *cultum*
"*animi*, the gifts and excellencies of the mind.
"And they are the same as those are of the
"body, beauty, health, and strength. The
"beauty of the minde is shewed in gratefull
"and acceptable forms and sweetnesse of be-
"haviour; and they that haue that gift, cause
"those to whom they deny any thing to goe
"better contented away, than men of con-
"trary disposition doe those to whom they
"grant. Health of mind consisteth in an
"vnmoueable constancy and freedome from
"passions, which are indeed the *sicknesse of*
"*the mind*; strength of mind is that actiue
"power which maketh vs perform good and
"great things, as well as health and even
"temper of mind keepeth vs from euil and
"base things. First, these three are to bee
"sought for, although the greatest part of
"men haue none of them. Some haue one
"and lacke the other two; some few attaine
"to haue two of them, and lacke the third;
"and almost none of them haue all.

"The first way to attaine to experience of
"forms and behauiour, is to make the minde
"itselfe expert; for behauiour is but a gar-
"ment, and it is easie to make a comely gar-
                                    "ment

" ment for a body that is well proportioned;
" whereas a deformed body can neuer bee
" helped by taylor's art, but the counterfetting
" will appeare. And in the forme of the
" minde it is a true rule, that a man may
" mende his faults with as little labor as couer
" them.

" The second way is by imitation, and to
" that end good choyce is to be made with
" whom we conuerfe; therefore your Lord-
" ſhip ſhould affect their companie whom you
" finde to be worthieſt, and moſt partially
" thinke them moſt worthy whom you affect.
" To attaine to the health of the minde we
" muſt vſe the ſame means which wee doe for
" the health of our bodies; that is, to make
" obſeruance what diſeaſes we are apteſt to
" fall into, and to prouide againſt them; for
" phyſicke hath not more remedy againſt the
" diſeaſe of the body, than reaſon hath pre-
" ſeruatiues againſt the paſſions of the mind.

" To ſet downe meanes how a man may
" attaine to the actiue power mentioned in
" this place (I meane ſtrength of mind), is
" much harder than to giue rules in the other
" two: for behauiour and good forme may be
" gotten by education, and health, and even
                                        " temper

"temper of the minde, by good obseruation;
"but if there bee not in nature some partner
"in this active strength, it can never be at-
"tained by any industry, for the virtues that
"are profuse vnto it, are liberality, magna-
"nimity, fortitude, and magnificence; and
"some are by nature so couetous and coward-
"ly, as it is as much in vaine to inflame or
"enlarge their minds, as to goe about to
"plough the rockes. But where these active
"vertues are but budding, they must be re-
"paired by ripenesse of iudgement, and cus-
"tome of wel-doing. Clearnesse of iudge-
"ment makes men liberal, for it teacheth
"them to esteeme of the goods of fortune,
"not for themselues (for so they are but taylors
"to them) but for their vse, for so they are
"Lords over them. And it maketh vs know
"that it is *beatius dare quam accipere*, the one
"being a badge of soueraignty, the other of
"subjection. Also it leadeth vs to fortitude,
"for it teacheth that wee should not too much
"prize life, which we cannot keepe, nor feare
"death, which wee cannot shunne; that as
"he which dieth nobly doth liue for euer, so
"hee that doth liue in feare, doth die con-
"tinually. I shall not need to prove these
"two things; for we see by experience, they
"hold true in all things which I haue hitherto
"set

"set downe. What I desire or wish I would
"have your Lordship to take in minde, what
"it is to make yourselfe an expert man, and
"what are the generall helps which all men
"must vse which have the same desire. I
"will now moue your Lordship to consider
"what helps your trauell will gaine you.

"First, when you see infinite variety of
"behauiour and manners of men, you must
"choose and imitate the best; when you see
"new delights that you neuer knew, and
"haue passions stirred in you which you
"neuer felt, you shall know what disease your
"minde is aptest to fall into, and what the
"things are that bred that disease. When
"you come into armies, or places where you
"shall see any thing of the wars, you shall
"conforme your natural courage to be fit for
"true fortitude, which is not given unto men
"by nature, but must grow out of the dis-
"course of reason: and lastly, in your trauell
"you shall haue great helpe to attaine to
"knowledge, which is not only the excel-
"lentest thing in man, but the very excellency
"of man. In manners your Lordship must
"not be caught with novelties, which are
"pleasing to young men; nor infected with
"custome, which maketh vs keep our own ill
"graces,

"graces, and participate of thofe wee fee
"euery day; or given to affectation, which
"is *a generall fault amongft Englifh trauel-
"lers*, which is both difpleafing and ridicu-
"lous. In difcouering your paffions, and
"meeting with them, giue no way, or difpenfe
"with yourfelf, refoluing to conquer yourfelfe
"in all; for the ftream that may be ftopped
"with a man's hand at the fpringhead, may
"drowne whole armies when it hath run
"long.

"In your being in warres, thinke it better at
"the firft to doe a great deale too much than
"any thing too little; for a young man, efpe-
"cially a ftranger's firft actions are looked
"upon; and reputation once gotten is eafily
"kept; but an euil impreffion conceiued at
"the firft, is not eafily removed.

"The laft thing I am to fpeake, is but the
"firft you are to feeke, it is knowledge. To
"praife knowledge, or to perfwade your Lord-
"fhip to feeke it, I fhall not need to vfe many
"words; I will only fay, where it is wanting,
"that man is voyd of any good. Without
"it there can be no fortitude, for all dangers
"come of fury, and fury is paffion, and
"paffions euer turne to the contraries;
"and

" and therefore, the most furious men, when
" their first blast is spent, be commonly the
" most fearfull. Without it there can be no
" liberalitie; for giuing is but want of auda-
" citie to deny, or else discretion to poyse.
" Without it, there can be no justice; for
" giuing to a man that which is his owne, is
" but chance, or want of a corrupter or se-
" ducer. Without it there can be no con-
" stancy or patience; for suffering is but dul-
" nesse or senselesnesse. Without it there
" can be no temperance; for we shall restraine
" ourselues from good as well as from euil.
" For he that cannot discerne, cannot elect
" or choose. Nay, without it, there can be
" no true religion; all other devotion being
" but a blinde zeale, which is as strong in
" heresie as in truth. To reckon vp all the
" parts of knowledge, and to shew the way
" to attaine to every part, is a worke too great
" for mee to vndertake at any time, and too
" long to discourse at this time; therefore, I
" will only speake of such a knowledge as
" your Lordship should have desire to seeke,
" and shall have meanes to compasse. I for-
" beare also to speake of divine knowledge,
" which must direct our faith, both because
" I finde my owne insufficiency, and because
" I hope your Lordship doth nourish the seeds

" of

"of religion which during your education
"at Cambridge were sown in you. I will
"only say this, that as the irresolute man
"can neuer performe any action well, so *bee*
"*that is not resolved in religion, can be resolved*
"*in nothing else.* But that civill knowledge
"which will make you doe wel by your selfe,
"and good vnto others, must bee sought by
"study, by conferences and observations.

"In the course of your study, and choice
of your books, you must looke to have the
"grounds of learning, which are the liberal
"arts; and then vse study of delight, but
"sometimes for recreation, and neither drowne
"yourselfe in them, nor omit those studies
"whereof you are to have continual vse.
"Aboue all other bookes be conversant in
"histories, for they will best instruct you in
"matters morall, politicke, and military, by
"which and in which you must settle your
"judgment. I make conference the second
"helpe to knowledge in order, though I finde
"it the first and greatest in profiting; and I
"haue so placed them, because hee that is
"not studied knoweth not what to doubt,
"nor what to ask. To profit much by con-
"ference, you must chuse to conferre with
"expert men, for men will be of contrarie
"opinions,

" opinions, and every one will make his owne
" probable. In conference bee neither fuf-
" picious, nor belieuing all you knowe, what
" opinion foeuer you haue of the man that
" deliuereth it, nor too defirous to contradict.
" I doe conclude the point of conference with
" this advice. that your Lordfhip fhould rather
" go an hundred miles to fpeake with *one*
" *wife man*, than fiue miles to fee *a fair towne*.
" The third way to attaine to knowledge is
" obfervation, and not long life, nor feeing
" much ; becaufe as he that rides a way often.
" and takes no care of notes or marks to di-
" rect him if hee come the fame way againe,
" to make him know where hee is if he come
" vnto it, he fhall neuer proue a good guide ;
" fo hee that liueth long, and feeth much, and
" obferueth nothing, fhall neuer proue any
" wife man. The vfe of obferuation is in no-
" ting the coherence of caufes, effects,
" counfels, and fucceffes, with the proportion
" and likeneffe betweene nature and nature,
" fortune and fortune, action and action,
" ftate and ftate, time paft and time prefent.
" Your Lordfhip now feeth that the end of
" ftudy, conference, and obfervation, is know-
" ledge; you muft know alfo, that the true
" end of knowledge is clearneffe and ftrength
" of judgement, and not oftentation, or abi-
                                        " lity

" lity to discourse; which I doe the rather put
" your Lordship in mind of, because the most
" part of noblemen and gentlemen of our
" time, have no other vse nor end of their
" learning, but their table-talke. But God
" knoweth they haue gotten little that haue
" only this discoursing gift; for tho' like
" empty vessels they found loud when a man
" knocks vpon their outsides, yet if you
" pierce into them you shall finde that they
" are full of nothing but winde.

" This rule holdeth not onely in knowledge
" or in the vertue of knowledge, or in the
" vertue of prudence, but in all other ver-
" tues. I will here breake off, for I finde
" that I have both exceeded the couenient
" length of a letter, and come short of such
" discourse as this subject doth deserue. Your
" Lordship, perhaps, may find many things
" in this paper superfluous, and most of them
" lame. I will, as well as I can, supply that
" defect vpon the second aduertisement, if
" you call mee to an account. What con-
" fusion soeuer you finde in my order or me-
" thod, is not only my fault (whose wits are
" confounded with too much businesse), but the
" fault of this season, being written in Christ-
" mas, at which time confusion and disorder
                                       " hath

" hath by tradition not onely beene winked
" at, but warranted.

" If there bee but any one thing which
" your Lordſhip may make vſe of, I thinke
" my pains wel beſtowed in all. And how
" weake ſoeuer my counſels bee, my wiſhes
" ſhall be as ſtrong as any man's for your
" Lordſhip's happineſs.

" Your Lordſhip's affectionate
" Couſen, E.
" <u>Greenwich, Janu.</u> 4th
" 1596."

" *Poſtſcript.*

" If any curious ſcholler happening to ſee
" this diſcourſe, ſhall quarrell with my diui-
" ſion of the gifts of the minde, becauſe he
" findeth it not perhaps in his booke, and
" ſaith that health and euen temper of mind
" is a kind of ſtrength, and ſo I have erred
" againſt the rule, that *membra diuidenda non*
" *debent confundi;* I anſwer him, the qualities
" of health and ſtrength, as I have ſet them
" downe, are not only vnlike, but meer con-
" traries, for the one bindeth the mind, and
" reſtraineth it, the other raiſeth and en-
" largeth it."

A Letter to the same purpose, by Sir Philip
    Sydney.

"My good Brother,

"You haue thought vnkindneſſe in me
"that I haue not written oftner vnto you, and
"have deſir'd I ſhould write vnto you ſome-
"thing of my opinion touching your trauell;
"you being perſwaded my experience there-
"unto be ſomthing, which I muſt needs con-
"feſſe, but not as you take it; for you thinke
"my experience growes from the good things
"which I have learned; but I knowe the only
"experience which I have gotten, is to find
"how much I might have learn'd, and how
"much indeed I have miſſed, for want of di-
"recting my courſe to the right end, and by
"the right meanes. I thinke you have read
"Ariſtotle's Ethiques; if you have, you
"know it is the beginning and foundation of
"all his works, the end to which every man
"doth and ought to bend his greateſt and
"ſmalleſt actions. I am ſure you have im-
"printed in your mind the ſcope and marke
"you meane by your pains to ſhoot at; for
"if you ſhould trauell but to trauell, or to ſay
"you had trauelled, certainly you ſhould
"proue a pilgrim no more. But I preſume
"ſo well of you (that tho' a great number of

"us

" us never thought in ourſelves why we went,
" but a certaine tickling humour to do as
" other men had done), you purpoſe, being
" a gentleman borne, to furniſh yourſelfe with
" the knowledge of ſuch things as may be
" ſerviceable for your country and calling:
" which certainly ſtands not in the change of
" ayre (for the warmeſt ſunne makes not a wiſe
" ma); no, nor in learning languages (altho'
" they be of ſerviceable vſe), for words are
" but words in what language ſoever they be,
" and much leſſe in that all of vs come home
" full of diſguiſements, not onely of apparel,
" but of our countenances, as tho' the credit
" of a traueller ſtood all vpon his outſide;
" but in the right informing your minde with
" thoſe things which are moſt notable in thoſe
" places which you come vnto.

" Of which as the one kinde is ſo vaine,
" as I thinke ere it bee long, like the moun-
" tebanks in Italy, wee trauellers ſhall bee
" made ſport of in comedies; ſo may I juſtly
" ſay, who rightly trauels with the eye of
" Ulyſſes, doth take one of the moſt excellent
" ways of worldly wiſdome. For hard ſure
" it is to know England, without you know
" it by comparing it with ſome other coun-
" trey, no more than a man can know the
" ſwinnelle of his Lorſe without ſeeing him

" well

" well matched. For you, that are a logician,
" know, that as greatnesse of itselfe is a quan-
" tity, so yet the judgment of it, as of mighty
" riches and all other strengths, stands in the
" predicament of relation; so that you can-
" not tell what the Queene of England is
" able to do defensively or offensively, but
" through knowing what they are able to doe
" with whom shee is to bee matched. This
" therefore is one notable vse of trauellers,
" which stands in the mind and correlatiue
" knowledge of things, in which kinde comes
" in the knowledge of all legues betwixt
" prince and prince; the topographical de-
" scription of each country; how the one lyes
" by scituation to hurte or helpe the other;
" how they are to sea, well harbored or not;
" how stored with shippes; how with reve-
" nue; how with fortification and garrisons;
" how the people, warlike, trained, or kept
" vnder, with many other such warlike consi-
" derations, which as they confusedly come
" into my mind, so I, for want of leisure, has-
" tily set them downe; but these things, as I
" have said, are of the first kinde which stands
" in the ballancing one thing with the other.

" The other kinde of knowledge is of them
" which stand in the things which are in them-
" selues either simply good, or simply bad,
" and

" and so serve for a right instruction or a shun-
" ning example. These Homer meant in
" this verse, *Qui multos hominum mores cognouit
" et urbes.* For he doth not meane by *mores*
" how to looke, or put off one's cap with a
" new found grace, altho' true behavior is not
" to be despised; marry my heresie is, that
" the English behaviour is best in England,
" and the Italians in Italie. But *mores* hee
" takes for that from whence moral philo-
" sophy is so called; the certainnesse of true
" discerning of men's mindes both in vertue,
" passion, and vices. And when he saith, *cog-
" nouit urbes,* hee meanes not (if I be not
" deceiued) to have seene townes, and marked
" their buildings; for surely houses are but
" houses in every place, they doe but differ
" *secundum magis et minus;* but he attends to
" their religion, politics, lawes, bringing vp
" children, discipline both for warre and peace,
" and such like. These I take to be of the
" second kind, which are euer worthy to be
" knowne for their owne sakes. As surely in
" the great Turke, (tho' wee have nothing to
" doe with him), yet his discipline in warre
" matters is, *propter se,* worthy to be learned.

" Nay, even in the kingdome of China,
" which is almost as far as the Antipodes
" from vs, their good lawes and customes are
" to

"to be learned; but to know their riches and
"power is of little purpose for us; since that
"can neither advance vs nor hinder vs. But
"in our neighbour countries, both these things
"are to be marked, as well the latter, which
"containe things for themselves, as the former,
"which seeke to know both those, and how
"their riches and power may be to us auail-
"able, or otherwise. The countries fittest for
"both these, are those you are going into,
"France is above all other most needfull for vs
"to marke, especially in the former kind;
"next is Spaine, and the Lowe Countries;
"then Germany, which in my opinion excells
"all others as much in the latter considera-
"tion, as the other doth in the former, yet
"neither are voyd of neither; for as Germany,
"methinks, doth excell in good lawes, and
"well administring of justice, so are wee
"likewise to consider in it the many princes
"with whom we may have league, the places
"of trade, and meanes to draw both souldiers
"and furniture there in time of need. So on
"the other side, as in France and Spaine, we
"are principally to marke how they stand
"towards vs both in power and inclination;
"so are they, not without good and fitting
"vse, even in the generality of wisdome to bee
"knowne. As in France, the courts of par-
"liament, their subalterne jurisdiction, and

"their

" their continual keeping of payed iouldiers.
" In Spaine, their good and grave proceed-
" ings; their keeping fo many provinces vnder
" them, and by what manner, with the true
" points of honor; wherein fince they have
" the mofi open conceit, wherein they feeme
" ouer curious, it is an eafie matter to cut off
" when a man fees the bottom. Flanders like-
" wife, befides the neighbourhood with vs,
" and the annexed confiderations thereunto,
" hath diuers things to be learned, efpecially
" their gouerning their merchants and other
" trades. Alfo for Italy, wee know not what
" we haue, or can haue to doe with them, but
" to buy their filkes and wines; and as for the
" other point, except Venice, whofe good
" lawes and cufiomes wee can hardly propor-
" tion to ourfelues, becaufe they are quite of
" a contrary gouernment; there is little there
" but tyrannous oppreffion, and feruil yeeld-
" ing to them that haue little or no right ouer
" them. And for the men you fhall haue
" there, altho' indeed fome be excellently
" learned, yet are they all giuen to counter-
" feit learning, as a man fhall learne among
" them more falfe grounds of things than in
" any place I know; for, from a tapfter up-
" wards, they are all difcourfers in certain mat-
" ters and qualities, as horfemanfhip, weapons,
" wayting, and fuch are better there than in

" other

"other countries; but for other matters, as
"well (if not better) you shall haue them in
"nearer places.

"Now resteth in my memory but this point,
"which indeed is the chiefe to you of all
"others; which is the chiefe of what men
"you are to direct yourselfe to; for it is cer-
"tain no vessel can leave a worse taste in the
"liquor, it contains than a wrong teacher
"infects an unskilful hearer with that which
"hardly will euer out: I will not tell you
"some absurdities I have heard travellers tell;
"taste him well before you drinke much of
"his doctrine. And when you have heard
"it, try well what you have heard, before
"you hold it for a principle; for one error
"is the mother of a thousand. But you may
"say, how shall I get excellent men to take
"paines to speake with me? Truly in few
"words, either by much expence or much
"humblenesse."

SIR PHILIP SYDNEY.

This cavalier was mortally wounded at the battle of Zutphen. As he was carried along the ranks, fainting with loss of blood and
                                                        with

with thirst, some one presented him with a bottle of water: on seeing a soldier lying gasping upon the ground, who cast a wistful eye at the bottle, he said, " Thy necessity, " friend, is greater than mine;" and gave him the bottle.

He was so beloved, that when the surgeon of Count Hallard, who attended him as well as his wounded master, told him that he was afraid he could not save the life of Sir Philip, he angrily replied, " Away, villain! never " see my face again till thou bring better " news of that man's recovery, for whose " redemption many such as I were happily " lost."

" Not long before he died, he called for " music," says his biographer, " especially " that song which himself had entitled ' *La* " *Caisse Rompue*.' * His brother came to him soon afterwards, of whom he took leave in these solemn words: " Love my memory; " cherish my friends; their faith to me may " assure you that they are honest: but, above " all, govern your will and affections by the

---

* The voluptuous St. Ivetaux, on his death-bed, desired his mistress to play an allemande of which he was very fond. " *Enfin*," said he, " *que mon ame passe plus doucement.*"

" will

" will and word of your Creator, in me be-
" holding the end of this world, with all its
" vanities."

" So general," adds his biographer, " was
" the lamentation for him, that it was ac-
" counted indecent for a man of quality to
" appear at court or in city in any light or
" gaudy apparel, the lofs of fo excellent a
" man being accounted a public lofs."

Sir Philip was indeed the great Mæcenas of his country in his time; " for," as Lord Broke fays of him, " his bounty was fuch,
" that there was not an approved painter, a
" fkilful engineer, an excellent mufician, or
" any other artificer of fame, that made not
" himfelf known to this famous fpirit, and
" found in him a true friend without hire;
" fo that he was the common rendezvous of
" worth in his time."

Sir Henry Sydney, Lord Deputy of Ireland, wrote fome directions for the conduct of his fon Sir Philip; with what fuccefs the confiant tenor of his excellent and energetic life will beft evince.

" Ufe

"Use great prudence," says he, "in the choice of a wife; for from thence will spring all future good or evil; and it is an action, like a stratagem of war, wherein a man can err but once."

* * * *

"Touching the government of thy house; let thy household be moderate, and according to the measure of thy estate; rather plentiful than sparing, but not costly; for I have never seen any get poor by keeping a moderate table; but some consume themselves through secret vices, and then hospitality beareth the blame.

* * * *

"Marry thy daughters, lest they marry themselves; and suffer not thy sons to pass the Alps; for they will bring home nothing but pride, blasphemy, and atheism: and if by travel they get a few broken languages, it will profit them no more than to have one sort of meat served up in different dishes. Neither by my advice train up thy sons to war; for he that sets his rest to live on that, can hardly be an honest or good
"christian,

"christian, for that every war is in itself un-
"just, except the cause make it just.

* * * *

"Above all things, tell no untruth; no,
"not in trifles; the custom of it is naught;
"and let it not satisfy you that the hearers
"for a time take it for a truth, for afterwards
"it will be known as it is, to your shame;
"and there cannot be a greater reproach to a
"gentleman, than to be accounted a liar.

"Study and endeavour yourself to be vir-
"tuously occupied; so shall you make such a
"habit of well-doing as you shall not know
"how to do evil, if you would.

"Remember, my son, the noble blood
"you are descended of by your mother's
"side; and that only by a virtuous life and
"good actions, you may be an ornament to
"your illustrious family; and otherwise,
"through vice and sloth, you may be
"esteemed *labes generis* (the stain of your
"family, one of the greatest curses that can
"happen to a man.

"Well, my dear Philip, this is enough
"for me, and I fear too much for you at this
"time; but yet if I find this meat is light
"of

" of digestion, and do nourish any thing the
" weak stomach of your young capacity, I
" will, as I find the same grow stronger, feed
" you with tougher food. Farewell! Your
" mother and I send you our blessing; and
" Almighty God grant you his, nourish you
" with his fear, guide you with his grace, and
" make you a good servant to your prince and
" your country!

"Your loving Father,

"HENRY SYDNEY."

SIR HENRY SAVILLE

was provost of Eton college. He was a very severe governor; and the scholars hated him for his austerity. "He could not abide wits," says Aubrey. "When any young scholar was " recommended to him as a wit, he would say, " Out upon him! I will have nothing to do " with him; give me the plodding student* : " if I would look for wits, I would go to " Newgate for them; there be the wits." Sir Henry was much esteemed by Queen Elizabeth; he read Greek and politics to her.

* A celebrated ambassador of our times was told how clever a boy his son was. "I would rather," said he, " you had told me how industrious he was."

MARY,

MARY,

QUEEN OF SCOTS.

This unfortunate princess, soon after she observed how fatally she had been mistaken in trusting to the friendship and kindness of Queen Elizabeth, wrote with a diamond on the window of the castle of Fotheringhay,

> From the top of all my trust
> Mishap has laid me in the dust.

The bishop who preached the sermon at the funeral of this ill-fated princess was despicable enough to say, in the prayer previous to it, in which he gave thanks for those who had been translated out of this vale of misery: " Let us give thanks for the happy dissolution " of the high and mighty princess Mary, late " queen of Scotland, and dowager of France, " of whose life and death I have not much to " say, because I was not acquainted with the " one, neither was I present at the other. " I will not enter into judgment farther; " but because it hath been signified to me " that she trusted to be saved by the blood of " Christ, we must hope well of her salvation; " for, as Father Luther was used to say, " many an one that liveth a Papist, dieth a " Protestant."

Mary is said to have written a volume of poems on various occasions, in Latin, French, and Spanish: likewise the ' Consolation of her long Imprisonment, and ' Royal Advice to her Son.'

The ENGRAVING that accompanies this article is made from a gold coin, representing the head of Mary, and of her consort Francis, the second king of France, in the Collection of the late Dr. WILLIAM HUNTER.

This unfortunate queen was long in the custody of the Earl of Shrewsbury, who appears, by the following letter, to have been ready, in case of any attempt to rescue her from captivity, to assassinate her.

" To the Queen Elizabeth.

" May it pleas y^r most excellent Ma^{ie}

" It appereth by my L. Huntyndon's let-
" ters to me, wherof I here send yor Ma^{ie}
" coppy, that suspycion is of some new devyse
" for this queen's lyberte, which I can very
" esly beleeve, for I am (as alwes before)
" plauded her frends every where occupye
" their heddes thereunto, I loke for no lesse
" than they cane doo for her, and provide for
" her fall te accordengly. I have her sure
" enoughe,

"enoughe, and shall kepe her forthe comynge
"at yo' Ma^ies comandement either *quyke or
"ded*,* whatsoever she or anny for her in-
"ventes to the contrare; and as I have no
"doute at all of her stelinge away from me,
"so if any forsabell attempte bee gyven for
"her *the greatest perill is sure to be her's*.
"And if I be yo' Ma^ies true sethfull servante
"as I trust yo' Ma^ie is fully prsuaded, be
"yo' Ma^ie oute of all doute of any her
"escape or delyvere from me by flight, forse,
"or any other waye w'oute yo' Ma^ies owne
"expresse and known commandemente to
"me, and therupon I gage to yo' Ma^e my
"lyfe, honour and all. God preserve yo'
"Ma^ie for many happy yeres longe and pros-
"perously to rene ouer us.—At Sheffeld
"Castell, the 3 March 1572.

"Yo' Ma^ies humble and sathefull servante,
            " G. Shrewsbury.
    " To the Quene's moste
        " excellente Majestie."

* " It is too easy to discover the meaning of these
" frightful passages," says the ingenious and humane Mr.
Lodge. " Behold Elizabeth, the wife, the pious, the
" happy Elizabeth of England, the envy of the world in
" her day, and the wonder of history in our's, introducing
" the mutes and the bowstring into a dungeon, which she
" had prepared for the reception of a princess who had fled
" to her for protection!" Lodge's " *Illustrations of En-*
glish History."

SIR THOMAS GRESHAM

was perhaps one of the most illustrious characters of which this great and distinguished country has to boast. He has shewn how a desire of gain and an ardour for science may accord together, and how that wealth, which, in the hands of a sordid and illiterate possessor, becomes mere dross, and loses its splendid colour*, may, in those of a man of a more enlightened and benevolent mind, emulate the glow of the diamond, and illuminate and benefit mankind.

Money has, indeed, in all times been supposed the sinews of war. Of the truth of this observation, the behaviour of Sir Thomas Gresham affords an eminent illustration:

* *Nullus argento color est, avaris*
Abditæ terris inimicæ lamnæ,
Crispe Sallusti nisi temperato
   Splendeat usu.   HOR.

Gold hath no lustre of its own,
It shines by temperate use alone;
And when in earth it hoarded lies,
My P****** can the mass despise.

A Genoese merchant, by name Regio, had, pending the invasion of this country by the Spaniards, twenty or thirty thousand ducats in the queen's hands in the Tower. Sir Thomas Gresham, knowing this, advised the secretary of state, Sir Robert Cecil, to have them coined into ready money, by which her majesty might be a considerable gainer, and enrich her realm with so much fine silver; and the repayment might be made by way of exchange, to her great profit; or she might take it up of the same merchant for a year or two, which he thought Regio might be glad of. This money, as he said, would pay her debts both at home and in Flanders, to her great credit and honour throughout Christendom. And further to recommend his advice by his own example, he sent to the mint in the Tower five sacks of new Spanish royals, to be coined for the use of the queen.

Sir Thomas (by his exertions) prevented the Duke d'Alva from raising the tenth penny upon the Flemish, and made him *quake*, as he said, for *fear*, at the queen's great credit, and the ready vent the commodities of England found at Hamburg. He was likewise the instrument of supplying the exigencies of the English

glish government by money borrowed from its own merchants, which had before his time been lent to it by foreigners, who had enriched themselves at our expence.

Sir Thomas was an excellent scholar; and, conscious of the advantages of a learned education in correcting the confined ideas of trade and enlarging the understanding, he founded a college in London, at a very considerable expence, for the support of professors in the seven liberal arts, as they were then called. His charities to the poor were extensive, his hospitality great; and his general liberality, where the interests and the advantages of his country and of his friends were concerned, might well entitle him to the honourable appellation of the Royal Merchant, a title more flattering than that of a great conqueror, as it diffuses those blessings which the other but too often destroys.

Honourable indeed as it has always been to the merchants of London, that they have been no less distinguished for their generosity than for their industry and opulence; witness the many hospitals that are amongst them, witness their kindness to their distressed and
unfor-

unfortunate brethren*, witness their pecuniary exertions on all occasions where the good of their country and the interests of humanity are concerned. Indeed, their ardour for enterprize, and success in their undertakings, appear to inspire their benevolence, and enlarge their charity, in proportion as they fill their coffers, and bring down the blessing of heaven upon treasure so ably and usefully acquired, and so nobly and generously expended.

* A grocer in the city of London, who died a few years ago extremely rich, and who came into the house as a common porter, lost a considerable sum of money by the imprudence of a debtor who had great dealings with him. The poor man sent to him upon his death-bed, and implored his forgiveness for having thus treated him, and assured him how heavy it lay upon his mind; adding, however, that there was still something that "weighed more upon his heart;" which was, the consideration that he left a young and beautiful daughter poor and unprotected upon the wide world. His benevolent and merciful creditor requested him not to let that circumstance distress him, for that he would take care of her as if she were his own child. He was as good as his word: he sent the girl to school, and afterwards, by a considerable sum of money which he gave with her, assured her a comfortable situation for life in a wholesale milliner's shop of great business.

LORD

LORD BACON.

This great man appears to have been one of the most candid philosophers that ever did honour to human nature, and to have more considered utility in his works than fame. "I have often," says Dr. Rawleigh, his chaplain and amanuensis, "heard his Lordship
"say, that if he would have served the glory
"of his own name, he should not have pub-
"lished his Natural History; for it may seem
"an undigested heap of particulars, and can-
"not have that lustre which other books cast
"into method have; but that he resolved to
"prefer the good of men, and that which
"might best secure it, before any thing that
"might have relation to himself.

* * * *

"As for the baseness of many of the experi-
"ments," says he, "as long as they are
"God's works, they are honourable enough;
"and for the vulgarity of them, true axioms
"must be drawn from plain experience, and
"not from doubtful. To conclude, this
"work of the Natural History is as God
"made it, and not as men have made it, for
"that it hath nothing of imagination."

What his Lordship says of music in masques may be well applied to that of our immortal Handel. "Let the songs be loud and cheerful, and not chirpings, or pulings. Let the music be loud, sharp, and well placed." The following extract from his Essays should be recommended to the modern French philosophers:

"I had rather," says Lord Bacon, "believe
"all the fables in the Legend, and the Tal-
"mud, and the Alcoran, than that this uni-
"versal frame is without a mind; and there-
"fore God never wrought a miracle to con-
"vince atheism, because his ordinary works
"convince it. It is true, that a little philo-
"sophy inclineth men's minds to atheism;
"but depth in philosophy bringeth men's
"minds about to religion; for whilst the
"mind of man looketh upon second causes
"scattered, it may sometimes rest on them,
"and go no farther; but when it beholdeth
"the chain of them confederate and linked
"together, it must needs fly to Providence
"and Deity."

Marquis d'Effiat, the French ambassador at the court of England, was very desirous to become acquainted with Lord Bacon. He paid his first visit to him whilst his Lordship was ill in bed and had the curtains drawn about him; and, on being thus received, he said to him, "Your Lordship resembles the "angels; we hear a great deal about them; "we are anxious to see them, and are never "able to have that satisfaction."

The Marquis, however, paid him a more substantial compliment by translating his 'Advancement of Learning' into French; and Lord Bacon called him his son*, and left him by his will

---

* *Letter of Lord Bacon to Marquis d'Effiat. Translated from the French.*

"My Son, Lord Ambassador,

"Observing that your Excellence not only treats of and "makes marriages between the princes of Germany and "France, but also between languages (since you have "translated my book on the 'Advancement of Learning' "into French), I have resolved to send you the book I "have last printed that I had reserved for you, but I had "my doubts respecting the propriety of sending it to you, "because it was written in English. But now for that "reason I send it to you. It is a new edition of my "Essays, Moral and Civil, but so enlarged and augmented, "as well in number as in weight, that is entirely a new "book. I kiss your hands, and remain

"Your affectionate friend, and humble servant,

"VERULAM."

his 'Book of Orisons, or Psalms, curiously
'rhymed.'

When some one mentioned to Lord Bacon a great reformation in the church of England, he answered, "Sir, the subject of which we "talk, is the eye of England; and if there "be a speck or two in the eye, we endeavour "to take them off; but he were a strange "oculist indeed who should pull out the eye."

He professed himself much pleased with the answer of an old man, who sold besoms at Buxton, to a spendthrift who wished to borrow some money of him: "Borrow of your "back, and borrow of your belly, my good "friend; they will never ask you for the "money; now I shall be plaguing you for it "all day long*."

Lord Bacon, as an † hypochondriacal man, no less than as a philosopher, had turned his thoughts

---

* The Arabian proverb says, "A man who wears finer "clothes than he can afford, is like a man who puts on "rouge whilst he has an ulcer that is eating him up."

† Many men of talents have had delicate constitutions, as Richelieu, Peiresc, Descartes, &c. Whether it be that, according to Shakspeare,

The

thoughts very much to the art of medicine. He advises physicians to exert their talents in endeavouring to find out specifics against every disorder of the human body. "Common " medicines," says he, " are rather accom" modated to general than to particular in" tentions. " I remember," adds he, " to " have seen in England a Jew physician, who " had been very conversant with the Arabian " writers on medicine, and who used to say, " Your European physicians are men of learn" ing to be sure; but they do not know how " to cure diseases by specific medicines; they " have the keys to bind and loose, and no" thing else."

" Lord Bacon," says Rushworth, " was " eminent all over the christian world for his " many excellent writings. He was known " to be no admirer of money, yet he had the " unhappiness to be defiled therewith. He

> The incessant toil and labour of the mind
> Doth make the mure, that should confine it in,
> So thin that life peeps thro', and will break out;

or that, from debility of frame, being excluded from the usual exercises and amusements of mankind, they look within themselves for that exertion so congenial to our nature, in the improvement of their minds, which is denied to them in external matters.

" trea-

"treasured up nothing for himself or his fa-
"mily, and died in debt. He was ever in-
"dulgent to his servants, and connived at
"their taking bribes; and their ways betrayed
"him to that error. They were profuse and
"expensive, and had at command whatever
"he was master of. The gifts taken by them
"were for the most part for interlocutory
"orders in Chancery. Lord Bacon's decrees
"were made with so much equity, that
"though gifts rendered him suspected for
"justice, yet never any decree made by him
"was reversed as unjust."

Lord Orford calls Lord Bacon the prophet of unborn science, which Newton was afterwards sent to reveal; and Cowley, more poetically, says of this great man:

> Bacon, like Moses, led us forth at last,
> The barren wilderness he past;
> Did on the very border stand
> Of the blest promised land,
> And from the mountain top of his exalted wit,
> Saw it himself, and shew'd us it.

GALILEO.

This great Philosopher having seen a telescope invented by Metius, a Dutchman, made another

another like it, and had the merit of applying to useful purpoſes what Metius diſcovered by mere accident. By the aſſiſtance of this inſtrument he firſt ſaw the creſcent of Venus and the four ſatellites of Jupiter, which he called the Mediceean ſtars, in honour of his ſovereign the Grand Duke of Florence. It were much to be wiſhed for his happineſs that he had been contented with obſerving the heavens; but he was anxious to purſue a ſyſtem of their motions, and he adopted that of Copernicus, who was ſatisfied with merely laying down his ſyſtem, and not mixing it with any thing that related to the Scriptures. Galileo took great pains to make either ſyſtem agree with Holy Writ. Denounced to the Inquiſition of Rome, 1615, he wrote memoir upon memoir to convince the Pope and the Cardinals that the ſyſtem of Copernicus was founded on the Bible. But a congregation of Cardinals, nominated by the Pope to examine Galileo's reaſons, declared poſitively againſt them, and he was forbidden to hold, either in writing or in ſpeaking, that the motion of the earth round the ſun was declared in the Scriptures. Cardinal Bellarmine, who delivered the ſentence, aſſuring him that he was not puniſhed, nor obliged to retract his opinion, but that it was only inſiſted that he ſhould be ſilent upon it, and teach

teach it no more in future, Galileo did as he was ordered to do till 1632, when having publiſhed ſome dialogues in which he maintained his former opinions, he was again cited before the Inquiſition, by which tribunal he was condemned to be impriſoned, and to recite the ſeven penitential pſalms once in every week for three years, as a relapſed ſinner. His ſyſtem was declared abſurd and falſe in ſound philoſophy, and erroneous in point of faith, as it is expreſsly contrary to the Holy Scriptures. Galileo, then at the age of ſeventy, was obliged to requeſt abſolution for having ſupported the truth, which he abjured as an abſurdity upon his knees, laying his hands upon the Goſpels, and repeating theſe words, " *Corde ſincero, ac fide non fictâ, abjuro,* " *maledico, et deteſtor ſupradictas errores ac* " *hereſes.*" Yet it is ſaid, that as ſoon as he roſe from the ground, ſtamping with his foot he exclaimed, " *E pur ſe muove*; yet ſtill the " earth does move." His confinement was ſo little ſevere, that he was lodged in a palace of Rome, and he was permitted to go on foot to Viterbo during the term of it. Galileo lived to the age of ſeventy-eight, and was interred in the church of Sante Croce at Florence. A magnificent monument was erected to his memory in 1727, oppoſite to that of Michael Angelo

Angelo. Galileo's works are in three volumes quarto. His Latinity is more claffical than that of his contemporary Lord Verulam, and his Italian works are faid to be written with great elegance and power of illuftration.

GROTIUS

was the friend and difciple, in point of political matters at leaft, of the illuftrious and unfortunate Barneveld, Grand Penfionary of Holland. After the execution of this honeft and intrepid patriot, Grotius was condemned to remain in prifon for life, and was confined in the Caftle of Louvenftein in 1619, from which he had the good fortune to efcape foon afterwards by the affection and enterprize of his excellent wife. She had obferved that his guards difcontinued the practice they once had of examining a trunk filled with linen, which was fent every week to be wafhed at the neighbouring town of Gorcum, and thinking to turn their negligence to fome account, advifed her hufband to put himfelf in the trunk, on the top of which fhe had bored fome holes, and prevailed upon him to remain in it in prifon as long a time as it would take

to

to carry it to Gorcum. This rehearsal having perfectly succeeded, she chose a day when the commander of the fortress was absent, paid a visit to his wife, and mentioned to her in conversation, that the health of her husband was so feeble that she was resolved to send away all his books in a trunk, to prevent his studying, which, she affected to say, had very materially injured his head and his eyes. The next day she placed her husband in the trunk, and two soldiers took it up to carry it off to Gorcum. One of them complaining of the weight of it, "I am sure," said he, " there " must be an Armenian in it," the name of a religious faction in opposition to the then government of Holland. " Indeed," replied Grotius's wife, "there are some Armenian books in it." The trunk is carried off. One of the soldiers however, having some suspicions from the agitation which he observed in the gestures and countenance of Madame Grotius, asked for the key of it; she pretended not to have it about her; he runs to the commandant's wife and desires to know what he is to do. She, having her suspicions laid asleep by what Madame Grotius had told her the day before respecting her husband's books, orders him to carry off the trunk and to ask no questions. The important load is carried safe to Gorcum, of which the subject soon quits his confinement,

ment, takes a waggon to Valvic, and arrives
safe at Antwerp.

Madame Grotius, hearing that her hufband
was fafe, owns the whole tranfaction to the
guards. She is confined a clofe prifoner by
the commandant, who inftitutes a criminal
procefs againft her. Some of the judges were
of opinion that fhe fhould be detained a prifoner inftead of her hufband; but the States
General, to whom this illuftrious woman prefented her petition, ordered her to be liberated
from her confinement. " Such a woman,"
fays Bayle, " not only deferves a ftatue, but
" even the honours of a canonization in the
" republic of letters; for to her alone we are
" indebted for the excellent and luminous
" works her hufband has printed, and which
" would never have efcaped the dungeons of
" Louventiein if he had paffed in them all his
" life, which his judges chofen by his enemies
" had determined."

The obligation which this great man had to
his illuftrious confort is commemorated by
him in his Sylva, in fome Latin verfes which
begin thus:

―――― *Multum debere fatemur
Uxori.*

" I had

"I had forgotten to tell you, that with
"respect to Grotius what you heard of his
"intention to attend the Huguenot ministers
"before his last journey to Sweden is false.
"He was not prevented from going thither
"on account of the precedence which he
"claimed as ambassador of Sweden at the
"court of France. That dispute happened,
"as you well know, at the beginning of his
"embassy, and not at the end of it. I know
"the contrary from M. Issali, who knew it
"from M. Bignon the elder, that he had pro-
"mised M. Bignon his great friend, that
"when he returned from Sweden he would
"make a public profession of the Catholic
"religion."

Le Docteur Arnauld, a M. Vaucel,
Nov. 2, 1689.

Lord Arundel possesses at Wardour Castle a fine whole length picture of this great man by Rubens. He is standing near a chest, in allusion, perhaps, to that in which his illustrious consort saved him.

DUPLESSIS MORNAY

says, in his notes upon the third volume of the History of Thuanus:

"Duplessis had great authority with the Huguenots. He was very earnest in his endeavours to place his lawful sovereign, Henry the Fourth, upon the throne of his kingdom; but when he changed his religion he reproached him very bitterly with his conduct; soon afterwards Duplessis was attacked by M. de St. Phal, and beaten so violently that he was left for dead. He made his sovereign acquainted with his disaster, and received from him this letter so honourable to them both:

"M. DUPLESSIS,

"I am extremely sorry for the outrage you have received, in which I participate both as your sovereign and as your friend. With respect to the first title, I will do justice to it for your sake as well as for my own. If I bore only the second title, you would have no friend whose sword would fly quicker out of the scabbard for you than mine, nor who would risk his life more cheerfully for you than me. Be convinced of this, that I will most punctually perform

" the office of sovereign, master, and friend
" to you.   " HENRY."

When Louis XIII. thought of making war upon the Protestant party, Duplessis thus addressed him: " Sire, it is always a mark of
" weakness when a sovereign makes war upon
" his subjects. True regal authority consists
" in the peaceable obedience of those subjects.
" It is established by the prudence and the
" justice of him who governs. Force of arms
" should never be employed but against a
" foreign enemy. The late King would have
" sent to school, to learn the first elements of
" politics, your new ministers of state, who,
" like ignorant surgeons, have no other reme-
" dies to propose than iron and fire, and who
" would have advised him to cut off a sound
" arm together with that which is in a dan-
" gerous state."

Duplessis wrote some very curious memoirs from 1572 to 1629, quarto.

JOHN GERARD VOSSIUS

was a man of infinite learning, and wrote many excellent books, as ' *De Origine Idolatriæ*,' ' *De Scientiis Mathematicis*,' &c. &c.

He used to write his '*Adversaria*,' or Common Places, on *one side* only of a sheet of paper; so that, as occasion required, he had nothing to do but to tear his papers, fix them together afterwards, and send them to the press without transcribing. This saved him a great deal of trouble, and enabled him to put his books together very speedily when he had procured the matter for them.

THE DUKE D'ALVA

had invested the city of Leyden to bring it under the yoke of Spain. The besiegers, understanding that there was but a small garrison in the place, were very pressing with the besieged to surrender. The latter answered them from the tops of the walls, that they knew the Spaniards were resolved to reduce the place by famine; but that they ought not to reckon upon that as long as they heard any dogs bark in the town; that when that food and every other failed them, they were resolved to eat their left arms, whilst they made use of their right ones; and that in fact when they were deprived of every means of subsistence they intended to perish sooner than to fall into the power of a cruel enemy. After this declaration

claration they made some paper-money thus inscribed, 'For our liberty.' This paper after the siege was most faithfully paid.

THE DUKE DE ROHAN,

being taken ill as he was travelling in Switzerland, sent for the most famous physician of the canton, who was called M. Thibaud. "Your face, Sir," said the Duke to him, "is not quite unknown to me, I think; pray where have I seen you before?"—"At Paris, perhaps, my Lord Duke, where I had the honour to be farrier to your Grace's stables. I have now a great reputation in this canton as a physician. I treat the Swiss as I used to do your horses, and I find in general I succeed very well. I must request your Grace not to discover me."

BARNAVELT.

After the death of this virtuous and intrepid Grand Pensionary of Holland, who suffered rather for reasons of policy, and for his opposition to Prince Maurice the Stadtholder, than

than for any thing elſe, his children entered into a conſpiracy againſt the Prince, were detected, and condemned to death. Their mother waited upon the Stadtholder to beg their lives. He told her, he was ſurprized that ſhe, who had never begged the life of her huſband, ſhould now requeſt the lives of her ſons. "My Lord," replied ſhe, "I did " not aſk the remiſſion of the ſentence of my " huſband becauſe I knew that he was inno- " cent; but I aſk the lives of my ſons becauſe " I am well aſſured of their guilt."

CARDINAL D'ESTE.

This magnificent prince of the church invited Cardinal de Medicis to ſup with him. After ſupper they played at primero for a conſiderable ſum of money, and the Cardinal D'Eſte had prime, which he concealed, and loſt his money to the Cardinal de Medicis. When he was gone, one of Cardinal D'Eſte's attendants obſerved to his Eminence, that he had really won the party. "So I had, Sir," replied he; " but I did not invite my brother " Cardinal here to win his money."

CHARLES

CHARLES IV.

EMPEROR.

A MERCHANT of Prague had lent a hundred thousand ducats to this Emperor. The day afterwards he invited him to dinner with many of his nobles, and treated them with great magnificence. During the desert he set before the Emperor a basin of gold, in which was his note for the money he had borrowed, and said, " Sire, all the other dishes are in com-
" mon for the rest of the company who have
" done me the honour to partake of my re-
" past. This dish is destined for your Sacred
" Majesty, and I request you to accept of
" what it contains *."

---

* A generous action of the same kind is told of that great actor Mr. Garrick. He had lent Mr. Berenger five hundred pounds on his bond; soon afterwards he was invited to dine with him on his birth-day to meet some friends. He sent his excuses in a letter that inclosed in it his bond, which he requested him to apply to the good cheer and entertainment of his company.

GENERAL

GENERAL STUPPA,

Colonel of the Swifs guards in the French fervice, was once told by one of Louis the Fourteenth's minifters, that if all the money the Swifs had received from the Kings of France were added together, it would pave the great road from Paris to Berne. " Per-
" haps fo, Sir," replied Stuppa ; " but at the
" fame time if you collect all the blood that
" the Swifs have fhed in their fervice * it
" would make a canal from Paris to Berne."

CASIMIR II.

KING OF POLAND,

was one day playing at hazard with one of his gentlemen of the bed-chamber, who on lofing

* Francis the Firft, King of France, when taken prifoner at the battle of Pavia, and carried through the field of battle, obferved to one of the Spanifh officers who conducted him, that all his Swifs guards had been killed in their ranks, and were lying dead near together. " If all
" my troops," faid the Prince with tears in his eyes, " had
" done their duty like thefe brave fellows, I fhould not
" have been your prifoner, but you would have been mine."

a great sum of money to him was so indignant that he gave him a box on the ear. He was immediately seized and condemned to lose his hand, but Casimir immediately revoked the sentence, and added, " I am not astonished at
" the behaviour of this gentleman ; not being
" able to revenge himself upon fortune, he has
" revenged himself upon her favourite. Be-
" sides, I go still further, and declare myself
" the only person culpable in this business;
" for I ought not to encourage by my ex-
" ample a pernicious practice which may
" cause the ruin of my nobility."

SIGISMUND,

KING OF POLAND,

was King of Sweden, and was afterwards elected King of Poland. After his accession to the latter kingdom he obliged himself to pass every fifth year in Sweden. Being engaged in several wars of consequence, he did not perform his promise; and, in some degree to remedy this, he appointed forty Jesuits (by which society he was governed) to perform his functions at Stockholm. This plan was so disgusting to his uncle Duke Charles and

the

the senate, that they resolved to destroy their newly-appointed governors. They fired, therefore, into the galleon that was bringing the Jesuits into the port of Stockholm, and sunk it with the crew which it contained. The Jesuits of the city of Stockholm, indignant at the treatment of their brethren, endeavoured to persuade the people to rebel; they were soon expelled the city, and Duke Charles assumed the reins of government.

GIUSTINIANI.

This senator of Venice having one day asked a Frenchman in what charter was found that Salique law which had contributed so much to the glory of France; "Signor," replied the Frenchman, "it is to be found at "the back of that act which gives to the "Venetians the empire of the Adriatic Sea."

A Doge of Venice having one day with great pomp and parade shewed the Spanish ambassador to that republic the treasures of St. Marc, he, affectedly looking under the tables upon which they were spread, exclaimed, " *Qui non ch' è la radice?*"

"Venice,"

"Venice," says Sir John Harrington, (notwithstanding we have found some flaws in it) "is the only commonwealth in the make whereof no man can find a cause of dissolution. For which reason we behold her (though she consist of men that are not without sin) at this day with one thousand years upon her back; yet for any internal cause as young, as fresh, as free from decay, or any appearance of it, as she was born. And whatever in nature is not sensible of decay in the course of a thousand years, is capable of the whole age of nature."

SIR GEORGE WHARTON.

"On Friday was sevennight My Lord (Earl of Pembroke) and Sir George Wharton, with others, played at cards; where Sir George shewed such choler, as My Lord of Pembroke told him, 'Sir George, I have loved you long, and desire still to do so; but by your manner in playing you lay it upon me either to leave to love you, or to leave to play with you; wherefore, choosing to love

"love you still, I will never play with you more."—*Thomas Cole to the Countess of Shrewsbury.* Lodge's "*Illustrations of English History*," &c.

BEN JONSON.

The leading feature of the character of this great comic writer was perhaps never better delineated than in the following letter from Mr. Howell:

Sir,

"I was invited yesterday to a solemn supper
"by B. J. where you were deeply remem-
"bered. There was good company, excel-
"lent cheer, choice wines, and jovial wel-
"come. One thing intervened which almost
"spoiled the relish of the rest, that B. began
"to engross all the discourse; to vapour ex-
"tremely of himself; and by vilifying others
"to magnify his own Muse. T. Ca. buzzed
"me in the ear, that though Ben had bar-
"relled up a great deal of knowledge, yet it
"seems he had not read the ethics, which,
"amongst other precepts of morality, forbid
"self-

" self-commendation, declaring it to be an
" ill-favoured solecism in good manners."

WILLIAM DRUMMOND,

OF HAWTHORNDEN.

" As he was a very wise and learned man,"
says his biographer, " so he was very pious
" and religious; *feared God, honoured the king,*
" *and did not meddle with them who were given*
" *to change.* He never thought religion con-
" sisted in peevishness or sourness of mind.
" On the contrary his humour was very jovial
" and cheerful, especially amongst his friends
" and comrades, with whom sometimes he
" only took a bottle *ad hilaritatem*, according
" to the example of the best ancient and mo-
" dern poets, for the raising his spirits (which
" were much flagged with continual reading
" and meditating); but he never went to ex-
" cess, or committed any thing against the
" rules of religion and good manners.

" He forgave particular injuries with a true
" Christian spirit; he bore the misfortunes
" and cross accidents of life which regarded
" himself

"himself with courage and magnanimity;
"but those of the public lay heavy upon him.
"In the short account of his life written by
"himself, he says, 'that he never endea-
"voured to advance his fortune, or increase
"such things as were left to him by his pa-
"rents.' Whether he foresaw the shortness
"of life and that he was not to enjoy it
"long, or contemned any thing that was
"toilsome to acquire or that was to be kept
"by base and servile means, he used always
"that saying of Picus de Mirandola in his
"Free Discourse, *Inter meos libros a puero
"usque et intra fortunam vivere didici, et
"(quantum possum) apud me habitans, nihil extra
"me, suspiro aut ambio.*"

Heads of a Conversation between Ben Jonson
and William Drummond *of Hawthornden,*
January 1619.

He (Ben Johnson) said, "That his grand-
"father came from Carlisle, to which he had
"come from Annandale in Scotland; that
"he served King Henry the Eighth, and was
"a gentleman. His father lost his estate
"under Queen Mary, having been cast in
"prison and forfeited; and at last he turned
"minister. He was posthumous, being born
"a month

"a month after his father's death, and was
"put to school by a friend. His master was
"Camden. Afterwards he was taken from
"it, and put to another craft, *viz.* to be a
"bricklayer, which he could not endure, but
"went to the Low Countries, and returning
"home again he betook himself to his wonted
"studies. In his service in the Low Coun-
"tries he had, in the view of both the armies,
"killed an enemy and taken the *opima spolia*
"from him; and since coming to England,
"being appealed to a duel, he had killed
"his adversary, who had hurt him in the arm,
"and whose sword was ten inches longer than
"his. For this crime he was imprisoned,
"and almost at the gallows. Then he took
"his religion on trust of a priest, who visited
"him in prison. He was twelve years a
"Papist; but after this he was reconciled to
"the church of England, and left off to be
"a recusant. At his first communion, in
"token of his true reconciliation, he drank
"out the full cup of wine. He was master
"of arts in both universities. In the time
"of his close imprisonment under Queen
"Elizabeth there were spies to catch him,
"but he was advertised of them by the
"keeper. He has an epigram on the spies.
"He married a wife, who was a shrew, yet
                                    "honest

" honeſt to him. When the King came to
" England, about the time that the plague
" was in London. He (Ben Jonſon) being in
" the country, at Sir Robert Cotton's houſe,
" with Old Camden, he ſaw in a viſion his
" eldeſt ſon, then a young child and at
" London, appear unto him with the mark
" of a bloody croſs on his forehead, as if it
" had been cut with a ſword, at which,
" amazed, he prayed unto God, and in the
" morning he came to Mr. Camden's cham-
" ber to tell him, who perſuaded him it was
" but an apprehenſion, at which he ſhould
" not be dejected. In the mean time come
" letters from his wife of the death of that
" boy in the plague. He appeared to him,
" he ſaid, of a manly ſhape, and of that
" growth he thinks he ſhall be at the reſur-
" rection.

" He was accuſed by Sir James Murray
" to the king, for writing ſomething againſt
" the Scots in a play called ' Eaſtward, Hoe!'
" and voluntarily impriſoned himſelf with
" Chapman and Marſton, who had written
" it amongſt them, and it was reported ſhould
" have their ears and noſes cut. After their
" delivery he entertained all his friends; there
" were preſent, Camden, Selden, and others.

" In

" In the middle of the feaſt his old mother
" drank to him, and ſhewed him a paper
" which ſhe deſigned (if the ſentence had
" paſt) to have mixed among his drink, and
" it was ſtrong and luſty poiſon; and to ſhow
" that ſhe was no churl, ſhe told that ſhe de-
" ſigned firſt to have drunk of it herſelf.

" He ſaid he had ſpent a whole night in
" lying looking to his great toe, about which
" he hath ſeen Tartars and Turks, Romans
" and Carthaginians fight, in his imagination.

" He wrote all his verſes firſt in proſe, as
" his maſter Camden taught him; and ſaid,
" that verſes ſtood by ſenſe, without either
" colours or accent.

" He uſed to ſay, that many epigrams were
" ill becauſe they expreſſed in the end what
" ſhould have been underſtood by what was
" ſaid before, as that of Sir John Davies;
" that he had a paſtoral entitled, ' The May-
" lord;' his own name is Alkin; Ethra, the
" Counteſs of Bedford; Mogbel Overberry,
" The old Counteſs of Suffolk; an enchan-
" treſs; other names are given to Somerſet,
" his lady, Pembroke, the Counteſs of Rut-
" land, Lady Wroth. In his firſt ſcene Alkin
                                    " comes

" comes in mending his broken pipe. He
" bringeth in, fays our author, clowns mak-
" ing mirth and foolifh fports, contrary to all
" other paftorals. He had alfo a defign to
" write a fither or paftoral play, and make
" the ftage of it in the Lomond Lake; and
" alfo to write his foot-pilgrimage thither,
" and to call it a difcovery. In a poem he
" calleth ' Edinburgh,'

The heart of Scotland, Britain's other eye.

" That he had an intention to have made a
" play like Plautus's Amphytrio, but left it
" off; for that he could never find two fo like
" one to the other that he could perfuade
" the fpectators that they were one.

" That he had a defign to write an epick
" poem, and was to call it Chorologia, of the
" worthies of his country raifed by Fame,
" and was to dedicate it to his country. It
" is all in couplets, for he detefted all other
" rhimes. He faid he had written a difcourfe
" of poetry both againft Campion and Daniel,
" efpecially the laft, where he proves couplets
" to be the beft fort of verfes, efpecially when
" they are broke like hexameters, and that
" crofs rhimes and ftanzas, becaufe the pur-
" pofe

"pose would lead beyond eight lines, were
"all forced.

"His censure of the English poets was this:
"That Sidney did not keep a decorum in
"making every one speak as well as himself.
"Spenser's Stanzas pleased him not, nor his
"matter; the meaning of the Allegory of his
"Fairy Queen, he had delivered in writing to
"Sir Walter Raleigh, which was, that by
"the bleating beast he understood the Puri-
"tans, and by the false Duessa the Queen of
"Scots. He told, that Spencer's goods were
"robbed by the Irish, and his house and a
"little child burnt; he and his wife escaped,
"and after died for want of bread in King-
"street. He refused twenty pieces sent him
"by my Lord Essex, and said he had no time
"to spend them. Samuel Daniel was a good
"honest man, had no children, and was no
"poet; that he had wrote the Civil Wars,
"and yet hath not one battle in all his book.
"That Michael Drayton's Polyolbion, if he
"had performed what he promised, to write
"the Deeds of all the Worthies, had been
"excellent. That he was challenged for in-
"tituling a Book, Mortimariades. That Sir
"John Davis played on Drayton in an Epi-
"gram; who, in his Sonnet, concluded his
"mistress

"miſtreſs might have been the ninth worthy,
" and ſaid he uſed a phraſe like Dametas in
" Arcadia, who ſaid, his miſtreſs, for wit, might
" be a giant. That Silveſter's Tranſlation of
" Du Bartas was not well done, and that he
" wrote his Verſes before he underſtood to
" confer; and theſe of Fairfax were not good.
" That the Tranſlations of Homer and Virgil
" in long Alexandrines were but proſe. That
" Sir John Harrington's Arioſto, under all
" tranſlations, was the worſt. That when Sir
" John Harrington deſired him to tell the
" truth of his Epigrams, he anſwered him,
" that he loved not the truth, for they were
" narrations, not epigrams. He ſaid, Donne
" was originally a poet; his grandfather on the
" mother ſide was Heywood, the Epigramma-
" tiſt; that Donne, for not being under-
" ſtood, would periſh. He eſteemed him the
" firſt poet in the world for ſome things; his
" Verſes of the loſt Ochadine he had by
" heart; and that paſſage of the Calm, 'That
" Duſt and Feathers did not ſtir all was ſo
" quiet.' " He affirmed that Donne wrote
" all his beſt pieces before he was twenty-five
" years of age. The Conceit of Donne's
" Transformation; or, Μεταψυχωσις, was, that
" he fought the ſoul of that apple which Eva
" pulled, and thereafter made it the ſoul of a

" bitch

" bitch, that of a she-wolf, and so of a
" woman. His general purpose was to have
" brought it into all the bodies of the he-
" reticks from the soul of Cain, and at
" last left it in the body of Calvin. He
" only wrote one sheet of this, and since he
" was made Doctor, repented hugely, and re-
" solved to destroy all his Poems. He told
" Donne, that his Anniversary was prophane
" and full of blasphemies; that if it had been
" written on the Virgin Mary, it had been to-
" lerable. To which Donne answered, " That
" he described the idea of a woman, and not
" as she was." He said, " Shakespear wanted
" art, and sometimes sense; for in one of his
" plays he brought in a number of men, say-
" ing they had suffered shipwreck in Bohe-
" mia, where is no sea near by 100 miles.
" That Sir Walter Raleigh esteemed more
" fame than conscience. The best wits in
" England were employed in making his his-
" tory. Ben himself had written a Piece to
" him of the Punick War, which he altered,
" and set in his Book. He said there was no
" such ground for an Heroick Poem, as King
" Arthur's Fiction; and that Sir Philip Sidney
" had an intention to have transformed all his
" Arcadia to the Stories of King Arthur. He
" said Owen was a poor pedantick school-mas-
" ter,

" ter, sweeping his living from the posteriors
" of little children, and had nothing good in
" him, his Epigrams being bare narrations.
" Francis Beaumont died before he was thirty
" years of age, who he said was a good poet,
" as were Fletcher and Chapman, whom he
" loved. That Sir William Alexander was
" not half kind to him, and neglected him,
" because a friend to Drayton. That Sir R.
" Ayton loved him dearly. He fought seve-
" ral times with Marston, and says, that
" Marston wrote his father-in-law's Preach-
" ings, and his father-in-law his Comedies.
" His judgment of stranger poets was, that
" he thought not Bartas a poet, but a verser,
" because he wrote not fiction. He cursed
" Petrarch for redacting Verses into Sonnets,
" which he said was like that tyrant's bed,
" where some who were too short were racked,
" others too long cut short. That Guarini,
" in his Pastor Fido, kept no decorum in
" making shepherd's speak as well as himself.
" That he told Cardinal Du Peron (when he
" was in France, Anno. 1613), who shewed
" him his Translation of Virgil, that it was
" nought; that the best pieces of Ronsard
" were his Odes; but all this was to no pur-
" pose (says our author), for he never under-
" stood the French or Italian languages. He
" said

" said Petronius, Plinius Secundus, and Plau-
" tus, spoke best Latin, and that Tacitus
" wrote the Secrets of the Council and Senate,
" as Suetonius did those of the Cabinet and
" Court. That Lucan, taken in parts, was
" excellent, but altogether nought. That
" Quintilian's six, seven, and eight Books
" were not only to be read, but altogether
" digested. That Juvenal, Horace, and Mar-
" tial, were to be read for delight, and so
" was Pindar; but Hippocrates for health.
" Of the English nation, he said, that Hook-
" er's Ecclesiastical Polity was best for church
" matters, and Selden's Titles of Honour
" for antiquities. Here our author relates,
" that the censure of his Verses was, that
" they were all good, especially his Epitaph
" on Prince Henry, save that they smelled too
" much of the schools, and were not after the
" fancy of the times; for a child (says he)
" may write after the fashion of the Greek
" and Latin verses in running; yet that he
" wished to please the king, that Piece of
" Forth Feasting had been his own."

As Ben Jonson has been very liberal of his censures on all his co-temporaries, so our author does not spare him: " For," he says, " Ben Jonson was a great lover and praiser of
" himself,

" himself, a contemner and scorner of others,
" given rather to lose a friend than a jest;
" jealous of every word and action of those
" about him, especially after drink, which is
" one of the elements in which he lived; a
" diflembler of the parts which reign in him;
" a bragger of some good that he wanted,
" thinketh nothing well done, but what either
" he himself or some of his friends have said
" or done. He is paffionately kind and an-
" gry, careless either to gain or keep; vin-
" dictive, but if he be well answered at him-
" self, interprets best sayings and deeds often
" to the worst. He was for any religion, as
" being versed in both; oppressed with fancy,
" which hath over-mastered his reason, a ge-
" neral disease in many poets. His inventions
" are smooth and easy, but above all he ex-
" celleth in a translation. When his Play of
" the Silent Woman was first acted, there
" were found verses after on the stage against
" him, concluding, that that Play was well
" named the Silent Woman, because there
" was never one man to say *plaudite* to it."

Mr. Drummond gave the following character of several authors:

" The authors I have seen," saith he, " on
the subject of love, are the Earl of Surrey,
" Sir

"Sir Thomas Wyat (whom, becaufe of their antiquity, I will not match with our better times), Sidney, Daniel, Drayton, and Spenfer. He who writeth the art of Englifh Poefy, praifeth much Raleigh and Dyer; but their Works are fo few that are come to my hands, I cannot well fay any thing of them.

"The laft we have are Sir William Alexander, and Shakefpear, who have lately publifhed their Works. Conftable faith, fome have written excellently; and Murry, with others I know, hath done well if they could be brought to publifh their Works; but of fecrets who can foundly judge?

"The beft and moft exquifite poet of this fubject, by confent of the whole fenate of poets, is Petrarch. S. W. R. in an Epitaph on Sidney, calleth him our Englifh Petrarch; and Daniel regrates he was not a Petrarch, though his Delia be a Laura; fo Sidney, in his Aft. and Stell telleth of Petrarch. You, that pure Petrarch, long deceafi, wooes with new-born fighs.

"The French have fet him before them as a paragon; whereof we ftill find, that
"thofe

" those of our English poets who have ap-
" proached nearer to him, are the most exqui-
" site on this subject. When I say approach
" him, I mean not in following his invention,
" but in forging as good; and when one matter
" cometh to them all at once, who quintessen-
" ceth it in the finest substance.

" Among our English poets, Petrarch is
" imitated, nay surpast in some things, in
" matter and manner: in matter, none ap-
" proach him to Sidney, who hath songs and
" sonnats in matter intermingled: in manners,
" the nearest I find to him, is Sir William Alex-
" ander; who, insisting in these same steps,
" hath sextains, madrigals and songs, echoes
" and equivoques, which he hath not; where-
" by, as the one hath surpast him in matter, so
" the other in manner of writing, or form.
" This one thing which is followed by the
" Italians, as of Sanazarius and others, is,
" that none celebrateth their mistress after her
" death, which Ronsard hath imitated. After
" which two next (methinks) followeth Daniel,
" for sweetness in ryming second to none.
" Drayton seemeth rather to have loved his
" muse than his mistress; by, I know not
" what artificial similes, this sheweth well his
" mind, but not the passion. As to that
              " which

"which Spenser calleth his Amorelli, I am
"not of their opinion, who think them his;
"for they are so childish, that it were not
"well to give them so honourable a father.

"Donne, among the Anacreontic lyricks,
"is second to none, and far from all second;
"but as Anacreon doth not approach Calli-
"machus, tho' he excels in his own kind,
"nor Horace to Virgil, no more can I be
"brought to think him to excel either Alex-
"ander or Sidney's verses: they can hardly
"be compared together, treading diverse
"paths; the one flying swift, but low; the
"other, like the eagle, surpassing the clouds.
"I think if he would, he might easily be
"the best Epigrammatist we have found in
"English; of which I have not yet seen any
"come near the ancients.

"Compare Song, Murry and Love, &c.
"with Tasso's Stanzas against Beauty, one
"shall hardly know who hath the best.

"Drayton's Polyolbion is one of the
"smoothest Poems I have seen in English,
"poetical and well prosecuted; there are some
"pieces in him, I dare compare with the best
"Transmarine Poems.

"The

" The seventh Song pleaseth me much.

" The twelfth is excellent.

" The thirteenth also:—The Discourse of
" Hunting passeth with any poet. And

" The eighteenth, which is his last in this
" edition, 1614.

" I find in him, which is in most part of my
" compatriots, too great an admiration of their
" country; on the history of which, whilst
" they muse as wondering, they forget some-
" times to be good poets.

" Silvester's Translation of Judith, and the
" Battle of Ivory, are excellent. He is not
" happy in his inventions, as may be seen in
" his Tabacco batter'd, and Epitaphes; who
" likes to know whether he or Hudson hath
" the advantage of Judith, let them compare
" the beginning of the fourth book, ' O silver
" brow'd Diana, &c.' And the end of the
" fourth book, ' Her wav'd Locks, &c.'
" The midst of the eighth book, ' In Ragan's
" ample Plain one Morning met, &c.' And
" after Judas, said she, ' Thy Jacob to deli-
" ver, now is the Time, &c.' His pains are
                              " much

" much to be praised, and happy translations
" in sundry parts equalling the original."

THOMAS SUTTON,

FOUNDER OF THE CHARTER-HOUSE.

" It is reported," says Fuller, " that Mr.
" Sutton often repaired to a private garden,
" where he frequently prayed, and was often
" overheard to repeat this expression : ' Lord,
" thou hast given me a large and a liberal
" estate, give me also a heart to make as good
" use of it! The character of Volpone, in
" Ben Jonson's Comedy of the Fox, is said
" to have been intended for that of Mr.
" Sutton."

GUICCIARDINI

was not one of those political writers who
declaimed from the closet. He had been engaged in active life, and as his Epitaph tells us,
" *Ejus negotium an otium gloriosius incertum,*
" *nisi otii lumen negotii famam clariorem reddi-*
" *disset.*"

" The

" The name of equality," says this acute historian, " perfectly understood, is one of the
" most just and advantageous things to a state.
" But then this equality must be taken in a
" geometrical sense and proportion. For, as
" in matters of tax and imposition, the best
" levy is not by the poll, but according to
" every man's ability; and as, in conferring
" dignities and offices, the best choice is ac-
" cording to every man's fitness and suffi-
" ciency for the place; so in the deliberation
" respecting matters of state, and in the de-
" cision of doubts of the greatest conse-
" quence, a person of the soundest judgment
" should have the greatest weight, and voices
" should not be considered by their number *,
" but by their value."

* Lycurgus, being asked by a friend why he did not make the government of Sparta a democracy, replied, " Make
" the experiment in your own family."

" *Multorum manibus res humanæ indigent, paucorum capita
" sufficiunt*," says one very wisely: " Human affairs want
" as many hands as possible; very few heads are sufficient."
" What a happy place," says some Frenchmen, " would
" this world be, if every one would mind his own business,
" and take care that the business should be suited to his
" talents and to his situation. The world would not then
" be pestered with schismatics in religion, shallow politi-
" cians, dull poets, minute philosophers, collectors of anec-
" dotes, or readers of them."

AMELOT

AMELOT DE LA HOUSSAIE,

in his celebrated account of the government of Venice, says, " The Venetians lost their " dominions in Terra Firma two centuries " ago by their irresolution. They did not take " their party till the allied powers had made " an irruption into their territory. It is," " adds he, " a miserable policy to give way " too much to a powerful and designing neigh- " bour, and to exhibit any marks of fear.

" A state can at best be but conquered; and " it is more likely to gain good terms for it- " self, if it meets its enemy sword in hand, " than if it tamely lays down its arms be- " fore it.

" Three Frenchmen," said he, " had en- " tered into a dispute respecting the govern- " ment of Venice; two had abused, and the " other had praised it. The state Inquisitors, " who at that time had their ears every where, " were informed of the dispute, and had the " disputants taken up. Two of them were " hanged by the feet, and the third was taken
" to

" to the prison to see the fate of his compa-
" nions. He loudly exclaimed, 'That he
" trusted the same fate was not to await him,
" as he had defended, not traduced, the go-
" vernment of Venice.' One of the state in-
" quisitors told him, that all that the Venetian
" government required of persons who lived
" under it, was to say nothing about it, and
" never to speak of it either in praise or
" blame *. You Sir," then turning to the
Frenchman, said he, " are merely sentenced
" to

---

* Nothing is so undecisive as disputes about the constitution of any country. It is often not to be found in the
statute laws themselves, but sometimes in the mere execution of them, in the opinions of the inhabitants, and
in the actual government of the country. England is a
mixed government, and may make upon paper either a monarchy or a republic, as those persons who consult its records
with a partial view may wish to make it; it really partakes of
each form of government, and its subjects may well rest satisfied with it, as a constitution that has afforded more general and more equal liberty to mankind than any other country that the world has produced; a constitution, of which it
was said by an enemy in Edward the Fourth's time, that the
public good was more considered in it, than in any other
government in Europe; and of which, in the reign of
George the Third, a fastidious and incensed republican exclaimed, " I see that in this country the *people* are respect-
" ed." It matters very little whether a machine that answers its destination perfectly agrees with the model that
was

" to leave the territory of the republic in
" twenty-four hours, on penalty of death, and
" have good reason to be satisfied with the
" mildness of your sentence."

JAMES THE FIRST,

KING OF ENGLAND.

It was said of this monarch, that he was

Maximus in folio, minimus in folio.

Hunting and school divinity seem to have been his favourite pursuits, pursuits, of which the chace is painful and dangerous, and the end of no importance.

" There is no news here," says Lord Leicester, in a letter to Sir Robert Cecil, " but a
" reasonable pretty jest is spoken of, that hap-
" pened at Royston. There was one of the
" king's spaniel hounds (called Jouler) missing

---

was laid down for it; and as all government is a mere matter of experience, if the practice is good, why be continually recurring to its supposed principles? " The effects of gun-
" powder," says d'Alembert, " are in total opposition to all
" theory; yet who (particularly in these times) doubts of
" the force and violence of them?"

" one

" one day. The king was much difpleafed
" that he was wanted; notwithftanding, he
" went a hunting. The next day when they
" were in the field, Jouler came in amongft
" the reft of the hounds; the king was told
" of him, and was very glad, and looking on
" him fpied a paper about his neck, and on the
" paper was written, ' Good Mr. Jouler, we
" pray you fpeak to the king (for he hears *you*
" every day, and fo he doth not us), that it
" will pleafe his majefty to go back to London,
" for elfe the country will be undoone, all
" our provifion is fpent already, and we are
" not able to entertaine him longer.' It was
" taken for a jeft, and fo paffed over, for his
" majefty intends to lye there a fortnight."
LODGE'S " *Illuftrations of Englifh Hiftory*," &c.

" The King (James) called for the arch-
" bifhop's * letter, and was merried at the firft
" as I guefled; when he came to the hiftory

* The archbifhop had written a remonftrance to his fovereign againft his hunting fo violently, and at fo much expence. Peter the Great was one day afked by fome of his nobles to hunt the wild boar with them. " Hunt, gentle-
" men," replied he, " hunt as much as *you* pleafe, and
" make war on wild beafts. For my part, I cannot amufe
" myfelf that way, whilft I have enemies to fubdue abroad,
" and obftinate and refractory fubjects to reduce at home."

"of the treasure, and the immoderate exer-
"cise of hunting, he began then to alter
"countenance, and in the end said it was the
"foolishest letter that he had ever read."

Chelsea college was designed by James the First for a college of Polemic Divines. Dr. Jortin says, with his usual sprightliness, "With a very small and easy alteration, it "was made a receptacle of maimed and dis- "carded soldiers. If the king's project," continues he, "had been put in execution, "the house would most probably have become "a house of discord; and 'peace within thy "walls' would have been a fruitless wish, and "a prayer bestowed in vain upon it."

DR. HUMPHREYS.

WHEN Queen Elizabeth was at Oxford, she held out her hand to be kissed by Dr. Humphreys, the head of the Puritan party in that University, and who had opposed ecclesiastical habits with great warmth. As he came near to her, she said with a smile, "Master Doctor, "that loose gown becomes you well; I wonder "your notions should be so narrow."

When

When Mr. Cartwright and some of the principal Puritans were brought before the Star Chamber, in 1591, for refusing to take the oath, and give in their answers to the accusations alledged against them for non-conformity, and libelling the established church, they were told by the great lawyers then present, " That " since less crimes than theirs had been " punished by condemnation to the gallies, or " *perpetual banishment* * (as they said by prece- " dents), they thought the latter to be the " fittest punishment in their case; so that it " were to some remote place, from whence " there might be no danger of their return, " nor of disturbing the peace of the com- " monwealth by their writing or otherwise."

* Banishment to another country seems to be the appropriate punishment of those who, discontented with the government of their own, endeavour, by speaking or writing, to make others as disaffected to it as themselves. The crime, however, should be completely proved; and partiality and prejudice should be most religiously excluded from the accusation and the conviction. In the republics of Greece this punishment used often to take place, and it is to this day inflicted by the laws of Scotland.

ABBOTT,

ABBOTT,

ARCHBISHOP OF CANTERBURY.

This excellent prelate was accused by the Duke of Buckingham of living too hospitably for an Archbishop, and of entertaining people who were not well affected to the Duke's person. He replied in this manner to Secretary Conway on the occasion:

" When King James gave me the arch-
" bishopric he did charge me that I should
" carry my house nobly, and live like an
" archbishop, which I promised him to do;
" and all that came to my house who were of
" civil sort I give them friendly entertain-
" ment, not sifting what exceptions the Duke
" made against them; for I know he might
" as undeservedly think ill of others as he did
" of me. But I meddled with no man's
" quarrels; and if I should have received
" none but such as cordially and in truth had
" loved him, I might have many times gone
" to dinner without company. There fre-
" quented me lords spiritual and temporal,
" divers privy counsellors as occasion served,
" and men of the highest rank, where if the
" Duke thought we had busied ourselves
" about him he was much deceived. Yet
" perhaps

"perhaps the old faying is true, *that a man
"knowing himself guilty of any crime, thinketh
"that all men that talk together do fay fome-
"what of him.* I do not envy him that hap-
"pinefs; but let it ever attend him."

The Duke of Buckingham feemed foon to forget the good advice the Archbifhop gave him on his being made gentleman of the bed-chamber to King James the Firft: " 1. Daily "on his knees to pray to God to blefs his "fovereign, and to give to *him* grace ftu- "dioufly to ferve and pleafe him. 2. To do "all good offices between the King and "Queen, and between the King and Prince. "3. That he fhould fill his Majefty's ears "with nothing but truth."

Abbott was a great favourer of the celebrated Petition of Right in 1628, and was one of the managers for the Peers in the Conference held on the occafion between the two Houfes.

~~~~~~

SIR JOHN LAMB.

The Bifhop of Lincoln, being defired by Sir John Lamb to proceed feverely againft the Puritans very early in the reign of Charles the Firft, afked him what kind of perfons they were

were. " They seem to the world," replied he, " to be such sort of persons as would not " swear, be guilty of fornication, nor drink; " but that they would cozen and deceive; " that they would frequently hear two sermons " a day, and repeat the same again too, and " afterwards pray, and sometimes fast all day " long." The Bishop then asked Sir John whether those places where the Puritans were did lend freely their money upon the collection of the loan; and being answered in the affirmative, " No man of discretion," replied the Bishop, " can say that is a place of Puri-" tans; and for my part I am not satisfied to " give way to proceedings against them."

CHARLES THE FIRST.

Anno 1647.

" THE King is still at Newmarket, very " pleasant and cheerful, and takes his recre-" ation daily at tennis. His Majesty seems " much to delight in the company and dis-" course of Cornet Joyce, who brought him " from Holmby, and sent a messenger to St. " Alban's on purpose for Cornet Joyce to " come to Newmarket." RUSHWORTH'S " *Collections.*"

How

How little with respect to liberty * the situation of the good people of England was bettered by the government of the Parliament, the following extract from the Glamorganshire petition will evince: "The committees did exact as a bribe twenty pounds of a reverend, learned, and painful divine, for sparing to make him a delinquent; and the committees did threaten a lunatic husband's wife to make her husband a delinquent unless she gave him thirty pounds, which the gentlewoman gave lest her husband should be troubled in that case; and another man saying, 'I pray God mend these times,' was threatened to be made a delinquent."

On the night before he was hurried away to Hurst Castle in the Isle of Wight, he had some conversation with the Duke of Rich-

* Not long before sentence was passed on King Charles the First, he said to the President, "I do conjure you, if you love that you pretend (I hope it is real) the liberty of the subject and the peace of the kingdom, that you will hear me before any sentence is passed. I only desire this, that you will take it into consideration; it may be you have not heard of it beforehand. If you will, I will retire and you may think of it; but if I cannot get this liberty, I do protest that these fair shews of liberty and peace are *pure shews*, and that you will not hear your King."

mond, the Earl of Lindfey, and Colonel Cook. The peers had recommended the King to endeavour to escape. The King requesting Colonel Cook to give him his advice, he said to him, "Suppofing, Sir, I fhould not
"only tell your Majefty that the army would
"very fuddenly feize you, but by concur-
"ring circumftances prove it to be fo; and
"that I had the parole, horfes ready at hand,
"a veffel attending me, and hourly expecting
"me. I am now ready and defirous to attend
"you; and in this difmal dark night (as if
"it fuited your purpofe) I can forefee no
"difficulty in the thing. The only queftion
"now is, What will your Majefty do?" The King, after a fmall paufe, pronounced this pofitive anfwer, "They have promifed me,
"and I have promifed them: I will not
"break firft."

The Duke of Richmond urging Colonel Cook to proceed, and to detail his reafons to the King, he with his leave went on: "Your
"Majefty, I prefume then, intends by thefe
"words *they* and *them* the Parliament. If fo,
"the fcene is now changed, your prefent
"apprehenfion arifing from the army, who
"have already fo violated the votes of Par-
"liament as to invade your Majefty's free-
"dom,

"dom, and testify their intentions by changing
"the single sentinel of state at your outward
"door into strong guards in your bed-chamber,
"which is in itself a confinement, and the pro-
"bable forerunner of a speedy absolute impri-
"sonment." The King replied, he would not break his word, and bade him and Lord Lindsey good night, and that he would go and take his rest as long as he could. "Which, "Sir," replied Colonel Cook, "I fear will "not be long." The King answered, "That "will be as it pleases God." The next morning the officers rushed abruptly into the king's room, and conveyed him to Hurst Castle.

Charles wrote the following lines on the blank leaf of a book in the Treaty House at Newport, in the Isle of Wight, 21st October 1648:

> A coward's still unsafe; but courage knows
> No other foe but him who doth oppose.

When Prince of Wales Charles was matriculated of the University of Oxford. Under the notice of his matriculation in the University book he wrote with his own hand:

> Si vis omnia subjicere, subjice te rationi.

He was so scrupulous of observing the rules of the University, that when he was at Oxford with his army he was desirous to have a book from the Bodleian Library to read at his lodgings. The statutes of the library were brought to him, and the keeper pointed out to him the prohibition of lending out any books from the library. The King was satisfied, and went in person to the library to read his book *.

When the vault, in which the body of King Charles was deposited in the collegiate chapel of Windsor, was opened to lay in a still-born child of Ann, Princess of Denmark, the coffin was found covered with a velvet pall, strong, and sound. A leaden band surrounded it, on which was inscribed

King Charles, 1648.

~~~~~

PRINCESS ELIZABETH.

" September 8, 1650, died Lady Eliza-
" beth, daughter to the late King, at Caris-

---

* The Bodleian Library was saved from being plundered by Lord Fairfax.

broke

"broke Caftle. She was a lady of incompa-
"rable abilities and admirable virtues; but
"being by the order of the regicides fent to
"the tedious prifon of her royal father, and
"more fenfible of his murder than the lofs
"of her own liberty, fhe wafted away, and
"expired with the extremity of melancholy
"and grief in the fifteenth year of her age."
Peck's "*Defiderata Curiofa.*"

ARCHBISHOP JUXON.

Lord Falkland faid of this excellent prelate, that he was the only perfon he had ever known who was not fpoiled by a pair of lawn fleeves. "It is a fingular ornament to "his character," fays Mr. Le Neve, "that "he fo plainly and fo honeftly gave the King "his thoughts about the death of the Earl of "Strafford, faying, that he ought to do no- "thing with an unfatisfied confcience upon "any confideration in the world."

JUDGE JENKINS.

This upright Judge had the honour to make collections for Lord Bacon. Being taken prifoner at the furprize of Hereford for
his

his defence of the cause of King Charles, he was carried first to the Court of Chancery, then to the King's Bench, and last to the House of Commons, the authority of all which places he denied. "His life was often "threatened, which he was always prepared "to lose," says Echard, "with a Bible under "one arm and Magna Charta under the "other. He spent his latter days in writing "a book called 'Lex Terræ confuted.'"

LIEUTENANT COLONEL JOYCE.

When this insolent and daring officer (then only a cornet) demanded admittance to King Charles at Holmby House, he said to those who guarded him, that his business was to speak with the King. "From whom?" demanded they; "From myself," said Joyce; at which they all burst into a fit of laughter. "Nay," said he, "it is no laughing matter; "I did not come hither to be advised by you. "My errand is to the King, and speak to him "I will and I must." When he gained admittance to the King his Majesty asked him by whose appointment he came thither. Joyce returned no answer. "Let then the commissioners
"have

" have their liberty," said his Majesty, " and " give me a sight of your instructions."— " Those," said Joyce, " you shall see pre- " sently;" so drawing up the greatest and best part of his army into the inner court as near as he could to the King, he said, " These, " Sir, are my instructions." The King took a view of them, and, finding them proper men, well mounted and armed, said with a smile to Joyce, " Your instructions, Sir, are in fair " characters, and legible without spelling."

It appears by ' Lilly's Life' that Joyce performed the office of executioner to Charles.

THOMAS TROPHAM

was surgeon to the Lord Fairfax, and was created bachelor of physic by the University of Oxford while Lord Fairfax, Oliver Cromwell, and the general officers were seated in their robes of doctors of law in the benches appropriated to the doctors in the Theatre. After the execution of Charles the First he was appointed to embalm the body and to sew on the head. This he did in the presence of many spectators, and exclaimed to them

them afterwards, that he had been sewing on the head of a goose *. Wood's "*Athenæ.*"

JOHN LILBOURNE.

The liberties of this country are much indebted to the exertions of this honest and intrepid man, who opposed the usurpation of Cromwell with the same spirit with which he opposed the violent and arbitrary measures of Charles's ministers. Persecution and cruelty had perhaps so sharpened and enflamed the mind of Lilbourne that he might occasionally see a grievance where there was none; and gave rise to the saying of the facetious Harry Martin respecting him, " that if there were none " living but himself, John would be against " Lilbourne and Lilbourne against John †.

---

* So far will party and prejudice go. Charles was assuredly the most learned, the most accomplished, and the finest gentleman of any of the monarchs that have blessed this country; and Harry Martin said in the House of Commons after his death, " that if we were to have a king, " he had as soon have the last gentleman in that situation " as any sovereign he had ever known."

† It was said of Don Carlos, the unfortunate son of Philip the Second of Spain, by a Spanish historian, " that " he was *Discordia, non homo*;" not a man, but the spirit of Contradiction personified.

JOHN HAMPDEN.

"Prince Rupert, in one of his excur-
"sions into Buckinghamshire, engaged the
"Parliament forces June 18, 1643, put them
"to the rout, and took Captain Sheffield
"and many others prisoners. Major Gunter
"was shot dead upon the place, and Mr.
"Hampden (one of the Five Members) who
"would needs go out with his party con-
"trary to the advice of his friends, not being
"ordered to it, was wounded and died thereof
"June 24, his death much lamented by the
"Parliament party.

"Dec. 17, 1647.
"An ordinance was read in the House of
"Commons, appointing the sum of 5000l.
"formerly ordered to the executors of Mr.
"Hampden deceased, to be paid to the assigns
"of the said late Mr. Hampden, out of the
"excise in course, the moiety of the receipts
"of Goldsmith's Hall, and the King's re-
"venue."—Rushworth's "*Historical Col-
"lections.*"

LORD

LORD STRAFFORD.

According to Rushworth, Lord Strafford marched to the block more like a general at the head of an army, as many of the spectators then said, to breathe victory, than like a condemned man to suffer death. The Lieutenant of the Tower desired him to take coach for fear the people should rush upon him and tear him to pieces. "No, no," said he, "Master Lieutenant, I dare look death "in the face, and I hope the people too. "Have you a care that I do not escape, and "I care not how I die, whether by the hand "of the executioner, or the folly and the "madness of the people. If that may give "them better content, it is all one to me."

"He recommended his son to be brought "up by the same governors to whom he had "committed him, and that he should not "change them unless they were weary of "him; but that he should rather want him- "self than they should want any thing they "should desire.

"He likewise recommended to him, as he "was on the scaffold, to bear no grudge to any
"one

" one concerning himself, and to be content
" with being a servant of his country as a juf-
" tice of peace, not aiming at higher prefer-
" ment.

" Lord Strafford was," fays his biographer, " naturally exceedingly choleric, an
" infirmity with which he had great wreft-
" lings; and though he kept a watchful-
" nefs over himfelf concerning it, yet he
" could not be fo prevented, but fome
" times upon fudden occafions it would
" break. He had fundry friends that often
" admonifhed him of it, and he had the great
" prudence to take in good part fuch admo-
" nitions. Nay, I can fay that I, one of his
" moft intimate friends, never gained more
" upon his truft and affection than by this
" freedom with him in telling him of his
" weakneffes. For he was a man and not
" an angel; yet fuch a man as made a con-
" fcience of his ways, and did endeavour to
" grow in virtue and victory over himfelf,
" and made good progrefs accordingly.

" I need fay little of his eloquence and
" abilities in fpeech. Both Houfes of Par-
" liament in England, and the Star Chamber
" and

" and Council Table there, as alſo the Pre-
" ſidential Court of York, and the Council
" Chamber, and Star Chamber, and Parlia-
" ment of Ireland; and as much as any of
" theſe his laſt defence at his trial in Weſt-
" minſter Hall, before the King, Queen,
" Lords, Houſe of Commons, and a multitude
" of auditors of all ſorts, are moſt full and
" abundant witneſſes thereof; to omit his
" public and private letters, which ſhewed
" that he writ as well as he ſpoke. This per-
" fection he attained, firſt, by reading well-
" penned authors in French, Engliſh, and
" Latin, and obſerving their expreſſions; ſe-
" condly, by hearing of eloquent men, which
" he did diligently in their ſermons and public
" ſpeeches; thirdly, by a very great care and
" induſtry which he uſed when he was young
" in penning his epiſtles and miſſives of what
" ſubject ſoever; but, above all, he had a
" natural greatneſs of wit and fancy, with
" great clearneſs of judgment and much prac-
" tice, without which his other helps of read-
" ing and of hearing would not have brought
" him to that perfection to which he at-
" tained. I learned one rule from him which
" I think worthy to be remembered: when
" he met with a well-penned oration or tract
                                    " upon

" upon any subject or question, he framed a
" speech upon the same argument, inventing
" and disposing what seemed fit to be said
" upon the subject before he read the book;
" then reading the book compared his own
" with the author's, and noted his own defects
" and the author's art and fullness; whereby
" he observed all that was in the author more
" strictly, and might better judge of his own
" wants to supply them.

" But amongst all his qualities none was
" more eminent than his friendship, wherein
" he did study and excel; a subject wherein
" I can worst express myself, though I have
" most to say and greatest scope to enlarge
" myself. For I cannot think of him without
" remembering what I lost in his death; a
" treasure which no earthly thing can coun-
" tervail; such a friend as never man within
" the compass of my knowledge had, so ex-
" cellent a friend and so much mine. He
" never had any thing in his possession or
" power which he thought too dear for his
" friends. He was never weary to take pains
" for them, or to employ the utmost of his
" abilities in their service. No fear, trouble,
" or expence, deterred him from speaking or
" doing any thing which the occasion of his

" friends

" friends required. He was never forgetful,
" nor needed to be solicited to do or procure
" any courtesy which he thought useful for
" or desired by his friends. He spent eight
" years time, besides his pains and money, in
" soliciting the business and suits of his ne-
" phews, Sir George and Sir William Saville,
" going every term to London about that
" only, without missing one in thirty, as I
" verily believe; and all this merely in me-
" mory of the kindness that had passed be-
" tween him and his brother-in-law, Sir G.
" Saville, their deceased father.

* * * *

" It will be too long for me to design or
" express the obligations his kindness laid on
" particular men. There are many that have
" cause to remember them, and they or their
" posterity enjoy the fruit thereof. In fine,
" he did not seek friendship with all men; but
" where he desired intimacy, his kindness did
" appear much more in effect than in words.
" He never failed where he did profess friend-
" ship, yet the time was when he might have
" secured himself from great opposition raised
" against him in Parliament if he would have
" consented to have done and forborn to have
" done

" done some things concerning some whom
" he accounted his friends, which some men
" would not have scrupled at; and God
" knows whether he was repaid again with
" the like kindness and felicity."

Lord Strafford, in the first speech which he made as Lord Lieutenant of Ireland to both Houses of Parliament of that kingdom, amongst other excellent advice which he gave them, says,

" Divide not nationally betwixt English
" and Irish. The King makes no distinction
" betwixt you, reputes you all without pre-
" judice, and that upon full and true grounds.
" I assure you, his good and faithful subjects;
" and madness it were then in you to raise
" that wall of separation amongst yourselves.
" If you should, you know whom the old
" proverb deems likest to go to the wall; and
" believe me England will not prove the
" weakest.

" Chiefly beware of divisions in your coun-
" cils, for division confines always upon
" ruin, leads ever to some fatal precipice or
" other. Divide not between Protestant and
" Catholic, for this meeting is merely civil,
" religion

"religion not at all concerned one way or
"other. In this I have endeavoured to give
"you satisfaction both privately and pub-
"lickly; and now I assure you again that
"there is nothing of religion to be stirred in
"this Parliament. For believe me, I have a
"more hallowed regard for my master's ho-
"nour than to profane his chair with un-
"truths, so as if any after all this shall again
"spring this doubt amongst you, it is not to
"be judged from hardness of belief, but much
"rather from a perverse and malevolent
"spirit, desirous to embroil your peaceable
"proceedings with party and faction; and I
"trust your wisdom and temper will quickly
"conjure all such forth from amongst you.

"Take heed of private meetings and con-
"sults in your chambers, by design and pri-
"vily aforehand to combine how to discourse
"and carry the publick affairs when you
"come into the Houses. For besides that
"they are in themselves unlawful, and punish-
"able in a grievous measure, I never knew
"them in my experience to do any good to
"the public or to any particular man. I
"have often known them do much harm to
"both."

PRINJE

PRINCE RUPERT.

"The Prince Elector went not home fo foon as I wrote in my laſt; he ſtayed for the ten thouſand pounds her Majeſty was pleaſed to give him*. Both the brothers went away unwillingly, but Prince Rupert expreſſed it moſt; for being a hunting he wiſhed that he might break his neck ſo, that he might leave his bones in England."— *Mr. Gerard to Lord Strafford*, 1633, October 9.

SIR DUDLEY DIGGES,

in his ſpeech at a conference between the two Houſes of Parliament, ſaid finely of the common law of England,

Ingrediturque ſolo, et caput inter nubila condit.

What tho' it walks the earth with ſolemn tread,
Yet in the clouds it hides its ſacred head.

* *Proceedings in the Iriſh Houſe of Commons*, 1798. The Committee ordered the report of the Duke of Mecklenburg's penſion to be brought up!

"The laws of England," added he, "are grounded on reason, more ancient than books, consisting much in unwritten customs, and so ancient, that from the Saxon times to those of the Danes, notwithstanding the injuries and ruins of time, they have continued in most things the same *."
"The Chronicle of Litchfield, speaking of the tyranny of the Danes, says, *Tunc jus sopitum erat in regno, leges & consuetudines Angliæ, sopitæ erant, prava voluntas vis & violentia regnabant, potius quam judicia vel justitia.* Yet by the blessing of God, a good king (St. Edward) did awaken those laws, or, as the old words are, *excitatas reparavit, reparatas decoravit, decoratas confirmavit,* which word *confirmavit* shews that good King Edward did not *give* those laws which William the Conqueror, and all his successors since that time, have sworn unto."

* In consequence of the connection between the Saxon and the English law, Dr. Rawlinson left a sum of money to establish a professorship of the Saxon language at Oxford. It has been, for these last two years, held with great credit by the ingenious Mr. Mayo, Fellow of St. John's College.

SIR EDWARD COKE.

Echard says, that "this great lawyer loſt "his preferment by the ſame means by which "he got it, by his tongue. His receſs," adds he, "was far from being inglorious; "and he was ſo excellent at improving a diſ- "grace, that king James uſed to compare "him to a cat, that whatever happened would "always light upon her feet." Finding a cloud at court, he met with fair weather in the country, where he ſo eſpouſed the cauſe of the people, that in ſucceeding parliaments the prerogative felt him as its moſt able and active oppoſer. We are told that the Duke of Buckingham would have reſtored him, if he would have given a gratuity, but he anſwered, "A "judge ought not to give nor take a bribe." He was an upright judge, and an able arguer. His uſual ſaying was, "Matter lies in a little "room;" an aphoriſm not often put in practice by the advocates of our times, who ſeem to wiſh to make an impreſſion upon their hearers

Non vi, ſed ſæpe cadendo.

COUNTESS

COUNTESS OF DERBY.

This intrepid lady, being summoned a second time by Lord Fairfax to surrender Latham House, in the Isle of Man, replied, "I have not forgotten what I owe to the "Church of England, to my prince, and "to my lord: I will defend the place until "I have either lost my honour or my life."

The Countess occasionally went out of the gates of the fortress, and often passed near the trenches. During the siege, she always began the day with prayer, and ended it with thanksgiving.

Colonel Rigby having one day sent her an impertinent summons to surrender, she exclaimed, "Tell that insolent rebel Rigby, "that if he presumes to send another sum- "mons within these walls, I will have his "messenger hung up at the gate."

ARTHUR

ARTHUR WILSON,

the   judiced historian of the life and reign of James the First, wrote the Memoirs of his own life under this title, 'Observations of God's Providence in the Tract of my Life.' The reasons that induced him to do this, he thus describes:

"Sunday the 21st of July, 1641, Mr. Beadle, of Bristow, preached at Leeze. His text was Numbers xxxiii. 1. 'These are the journies of the children of Israel:' insisting upon this, that every christian ought to keep a record of his own actions and wayes, being full of dangers and hazards, that God might have the glory.

* * * *

"This made me run back to the beginning of my life, assisted by my memorie, and some small notes, wherein I have given a true, though a mere delineation of eight and forty years progresse in the world. Wherein I never was arrested, nor arrested any man, never sued any man, nor was sued by any man (except in that particular
"of

" of Mr. King), never was examined nor
" brought before a magistrate, never tooke
" oath but the oath of allegiance, never bore
" witness, nor was called to bear witness in
" any business. So that though I lived in
" the world, I was not beaten with the tem-
" pests of it, shrouding myselfe under those
" goodly cedars, my two noble masters *,
" whose actions deserve an everlasting monu-
" ment."

The peculiar felicity of Mr. Wilson indeed merited his gratitude and his remembrance. Yet were many persons of less talents and less consequence to write the Memoirs of their own lives, posterity would be instructed, and mankind would become wiser and better than they are; then

—————— —— —— —— omnis
Volucrâ pateat veluti descripta tabellâ
Vita hominis: ——

The commerce of real life would then from actual facts and incidents supply that fund of information and amusement for which we in vain seek in fictitious histories; and, in the words of Lord Bacon, " bring home to our

* The Earls of Essex and Warwick.

" busi-

"business and bosoms" the experience of others. The French abound with these useful records.

OLIVER CROMWELL.

Lord Loudoun, Lord Chancellor of Scotland, in the consultation with Lord Essex and others respecting the removal of Oliver Cromwell from his command in the army, and proceeding against him as an incendiary, thus addressed Whitlock and Maynard: " Now
" the matter is (wherein we desire your opi-
" nions), what you take the meaning of this
" word incendiary to be, and whether Lieu-
" tenant-General Cromwell be not like an in-
" cendiary as is meant thereby; and which
" way would be best to proceed against him,
" if he be proved to be sik an incendiary,
" and that will clepe his wings from soaring
" to the prejudice of our cause. Now you
" may ken that by our law in Scotland we
" clepe him an incendiary*, whay kindleth
" coals of contention and raiseth differences
" in the state to the public damage, and he

* By an old law of Scotland persons of this description are banished beyond seas.

" is

" is *tanquam publicus hostis patriæ*, a public
" enemy of his country. Whether your law
" be the same or not, ye ken best, who are
" mickle learned therein, and therefore with
" the favour of his excellence we desire your
" judgment in these points."

Soon after the commencement of the struggles between Charles the First and the parliament of England, the following eloquent and impressive proclamation was set forth, which but too plainly shews the truth of the learned and sagacious Pascal's remark, " That
" of all human evils a civil war is the most
" dreadful."

" *Ordinance of the Lords and Commons touching*
" *Stage Plays. Sept.* 2, 1642.

" Whereas the distressed state of Ireland,
" *steeped in her own blood,* and the distracted
" estate of England, *threatened with a cloud*
" *of blood* by a civil war, call for all possible
" means to appease and avert the wrath of
" God appearing in these judgments; amongst
" which fasting and praying having been often
" tryed to be very effectual, have been lately
" and are still enjoyned; and whereas public
" sports do not well agree with public cala-
                                " mities,

" mities, nor public stage plays with the
" seasons of humiliation; this being an exer-
" cise of sad and pious solemnity, and the
" other being spectacles of pleasure too com-
" monly expressing lascivious mirth and le-
" vity: it is therefore thought fit and or-
" dained by the Lords and Commons in this
" parliament assembled, that whilst these sad
" causes and set times of humiliation do con-
" tinue, public stage plays shall cease and
" be forborn. Instead of which are recom-
" mended to the people of this land the pro-
" fitable and seasonable considerations of re-
" pentance, reconciliation, and peace with
" God, which probably may produce out-
" ward peace and prosperity, and bring again
" times of joy and gladness to these nations."

It is said by Echard, that " Oliver Cromwell
" was particularly afflicted with the death of
" his old friend and ally the Earl of Warwick.
" But what chiefly broke his mind, was the
" death of his daughter Claypole, who had
" always been his greatest joy and delight,
" and who in her sickness (which was an in-
" ward imposthume in her loins) had several
" discourses with him, which inwardly per-
" plexed him, though none was near enough
" to hear the particulars; yet by her frequent

" mentioning in her agonies the blood her
" father had fpilt, particularly that of Dr.
" Hewett, people conclude that fhe had
" prefented his worft actions to his confide-
" ration."

But perhaps what more than all embittered the Ufurper's laft days was the publication of Colonel Titus's pamphlet of 'Killing no Murder,' which excited his countrymen " to run down and deftroy him as a " wild beaft, as *humani generis prædonem*."

" *Neceffe eft, ut multos timeat, quem multi* " *timent*," fays Publius Laberius to Julius Cæfar :

" He who fears many, is by many fear'd ;"

and the fentence was received with applaufe by the Roman people.

Could any thing deter mankind from indulging ambition, the following defcription of the ftate of anxiety and trepidation in which Ariftippus the tyrant of Argos, according to Plutarch, paffed his life after he had gained poffeffion of defpotic power and regal ftate, which are fo generally admired, extolled, and envied, as the height of human happinefs:

" The

"The tyrant, who had Antigonus for his friend and ally, who maintained so many troops for the security of his person, and who had taken care not to leave one of his enemies alive in the city, would not suffer his guards to do duty in his palace, but in several stations round about it. As soon as his supper was over, he sent away all his servants, fastened the doors himself, and then ascended with his concubine to a little chamber above, through a trap-door, on which he placed his bed, and slept (as a man in his condition may be supposed to sleep), full of fear, terror, and anxiety. An old woman, the mother of his concubine, every night removed the ladder by which he climbed into his bedchamber, and locked it up in another room. In the morning she brought it in again, and called up this happy, this wonderful tyrant, who came crawling out like a serpent from his hole."

In this example, as in many others, history too often spreads her instructive page in vain, to warn mankind of the fatal consequences attendant on the indulgence of ambition and other strong passions. The gratification of the present moment prevails over any considerations respecting the future; and we add one more example in our turn for the instruction of mankind, from which we may be tolerably certain they will not profit. Robespierres and Marats will still arise, and with their own blood make a scanty atonement for that of others which their ambition had caused to be shed.

FRANCIS,

EARL OF BEDFORD.

"This nobleman," says Lord Clarendon, "was a wise man, and of too plentiful a fortune to wish the subversion of government*; and it quickly appeared that he only intended to make himself and his friends great at court, and not at all to lessen the court itself." Indignation and

* "I pardon," says Xenophon in his Account of the Republic of Athens, "the people for being attached to a popular government; for is it not allowable to endeavour to do good to one's self? But if I see a man of high birth, who likes better to live in a democracy than in an oligarchy, I shall always suppose that he has criminal views, being well convinced that it is much easier for a man who has done wrong to remain concealed in a democratic than in an oligarchic government."

pique,

pique, however, make the wifeft perfons do ftrange things, and hurt themfelves and others very materially: the froward child, whofe hurt is occafioned, as he thinks, by the ground, and not by himfelf, is not contented till he has beaten that ground, however his efforts contribute to do greater mifchief to himfelf.

Lord Leicefter, in his 'State Papers', calls the Earl of Bedford by the name of " Higgledy " Piggledy," upfide down, every thing in confufion.

JOHN EVERARD.

" THE Council of State," fays Whitelock, " had intelligence of new levellers at St. " Margaret's-Hill, near Cobham, in Surry; " that they digged up the ground and fowed " it with roots and beans; and that John Eve- " rard, once of the army, and who termed " himfelf a prophet, was the chief of them; " that they were about thirty men, and that " they faid they fhould foon be four thou- " fand. They invited all to come in and help " them, and promifed them meat, drink, and " clothes. They threatened to pull down " park pales and to lay all open; and affured
" the

" the neighbours that they would shortly make
" them come up to the hills and work.

" Everard came to Lieutenant-General
" Cromwell, and made this declaration to
" justify their proceedings: He said, that
" he was of the race of the Jews; that all
" the liberties of the people of England
" were lost by the coming-in of William the
" Conqueror; and that ever since the people
" of God had lived under tyranny and op-
" pression worse than that of their forefathers
" under the Egyptians.

" But that now the time of the deliverance
" was at hand, and that God would bring his
" people out of this slavery, and restore them
" to their freedom in enjoying the fruits and
" the benefits of the earth.

" That there had lately appeared to him a
" vision, which bade him arise, dig, and plough
" the earth, and receive the fruits thereof;
" and that their intention was to restore the
" creation to its former condition.

" That as God had promised to make the
" barren land fruitful, so now what they did
" was to renew the ancient community of the
" enjoying

"enjoying the fruits of the earth, and to dis-
"tribute the benefit thereof to the poor and
"needy, and to feed the hungry, and clothe
"the naked.

"That they intend not to meddle with any
"man's property, nor to break down any
"pales or inclosures, but only to meddle with
"what is common and untilled, and to make
"it fruitful for the use of man; and that the
"time shall soon be, in which all men shall
"willingly come in and give up their lands
"and estates, and submit themselves to this
"community. And that for those who will
"come in and work, they shall have meat,
"drink, and clothes (which is all that is ne-
"cessary for the life of man); and that for
"money there was no need of it, nor of
"clothes more than to cover nakedness *.

"That they will not defend themselves by
"arms, but will submit to authority, and wait

* A few years ago Mrs. White and her followers, in Scotland, went out and preached the same doctrines, and observed the same practices. They lived out in the field in common, and held a community of goods. This lasted one summer; but on the approach of winter they parted, finding it necessary in those northern countries to live in houses, and that the soil was too ungrateful to produce without the mutual and varied labour of its inhabitants.

"till

"till the promised opportunity be offered, which they conceive to be near at hand; and that as their forefathers lived in tents, so it would be suitable to their descendants now to live in them.

"While these fanatics were before Cromwell, they stood with their hats on; and being asked the reason of it, they replied, Because he was but their fellow-creature.' Being then asked the meaning of that place in scripture, 'Give honour to whom honour is due,' they replied, ' That their mouths should be stopped who gave them that offence.'

"This," adds Whitelock, " is set down the more largely, because it was the beginning of the appearance of this opinion, and that we might the better understand and avoid those weak persuasions."

LADY DAVIES,

the widow of the Attorney-General of Ireland, having spoken something relative to Villiers, the first Duke of Buckingham, that
he

he should not be alive till the end of August, (which really happened) got the reputation of a cunning woman amongst the common people. She then became so mad, that she fancied the spirit of the prophet Daniel was infused into her, and this she grounded on an anagram which she made of her own name, Eleanor Davies, " Reveal O Daniel;" and though the anagram had too much by an *L*, and too little by an *S*, yet she found " Daniel" and " reveal" in it. For this she was brought before the High Commission Court; but whilst the bishops and the divines were reasoning the point with her out of the Holy Scriptures, Lamb, the Dean of the Arches, took a pen in his hand, and wrote the following exact anagram upon her name, " Dame Eleanor Davies, " *never so mad a ladie*," which having been proved to be true, by the rules of art, " Ma-" dam," said he, " I see you build much on " anagrams; I have found out one which I hope " will fit you." Having read it aloud, he gave it into her hands. This put the grave court into such a laughter, and the poor weak woman into such a confusion, that she afterwards grew wiser, or became less regarded. HEYLIN's *Life of Laud.*

LAUD,

ARCHBISHOP OF CANTERBURY.

The Commons, in their accusations against this Prelate, charged him with setting up and repairing Pope's images and pictures in the windows of his chapel at Lambeth. Amongst other topics of defence, the archbishop insisted, that the Homilies allow an historical use of images, and that Calvin himself allows them in this sense. See his 'Institutes,' b. 1. cap. 11. sect. 12. beginning *neque tamen eâ superstitione teneor*; and that the primitive Christians approved and had the pictures of Christ himself; Tertullian recording that they had the picture of Christ engraven on their chalices, in form of a shepherd carrying home the lost sheep on his back.

Laud, when bishop of London, attended Charles the First at his coronation as King of Scotland. It was observed, that Laud was high in his carriage upon this occasion, taking upon him the order and management of the ceremony. Spottiswode, archbishop of St. Andrew's, being placed on the king's right hand, and Lindsey, archbishop of Glasgow, on his left, Laud took Glasgow and thrust him
from

from the king with thefe words: "Are you a Church-man, and want the coat of your order?" (a rich cope, which he refufed to wear," fays Rufhworth, "as being a moderate Church-man"), and put the bifhop of Roffe at the king's left hand inftead of him.

~~~~~

SAMUEL TORSHILL,

in an Effay of his inferted in the Phœnix, and addreffed to both houfes of Parliament, recommends the difpofing the Bible into a method and harmony, by tranfpofing the order of books and chapters, inferting the facred oracles according to the times in which they were delivered, and the Pfalms in their places, or on thofe occafions, which they were framed to fuit; in fuch a manner, that by the mere force of feries and connection, the hiftorical and prophetical parts might reciprocally explain and illuftrate each other.

ARCHBISHOP

ARCHBISHOP USHER.

In a book belonging to this learned prelate was the following entry made with his own hand: " The King (Charles I.) once in the " prefence of George Duke of Buckingham, " told me of his own accord, that he never " loved Popery in all his life; but that he never " detefted it before his going into Spain."

Dr. Ufher was charged by his enemies with advifing his fovereign to confent to the death of the Earl of Strafford. " That is falfe," faid Charles one day to fome one who had made that accufation againft him to the King; " for " after Lord Strafford's bill of attainder was " paffed, the Archbifhop came to me with tears " in his eyes and faid, ' Oh, Sir, what have " you done? I fear that this act may prove a " great trouble to your confcience; and I " pray God that your Majefty may never " fuffer by the figning of the bill."

" The Archbifhop," fays his biographer, " lived at my Lady Peterborough's houfe near " Charing Crofs; and on the day that King " Charles was put to death got upon the leads, " at the defire of fome of his friends, to fee

his

"his beloved sovereign for the last time.
"When he came upon the leads the King
"was in his speech; he stood motionless for
"some time and sighed, and then, lifting up
"his eyes full of tears to heaven, seemed to
"pray very earnestly. But when his Majesty
"had done speaking, and had pulled off his
"cloak and doublet, and stood stripped in his
"waistcoat, and that the villains in vizards be-
"gan to put up his hair, the good Bishop, no
"longer able to endure so horrible a sight,
"grew pale and began to faint; so that if he
"had not been observed by his own servant
"and others that had stood near him he had
"fainted away. So they presently carried him
"down and laid him upon his bed."

Cromwell (at the intercession of the Archbishop, for whom he had a great respect) had promised to permit the ministers of the Church of England the freedom of their mode of divine worship in private congregations. The Archbishop waited upon him to claim his promise, which had not been performed, and found him under the hands of his surgeon, who was dressing a great bile which he had on his breast. Cromwell said to him, " If this " core, Sir," pointing to it, " were once out. " I should be well." To whom Dr. Usher replied, " I doubt the core lies deeper; there
" is

"is a core that lies at the heart that muſt be taken out, or elſe it will not be well."—"Ah," replied Cromwell, "ſo there is indeed," and ſighed. The Biſhop not ſucceeding in his application returned home, where he met with ſome of his friends, to whom he ſaid, "This falſe man hath broken his word with me, and refuſes to perform what he promiſed. Well, he will have little cauſe to glory in his wickedneſs, for he will not continue long; the King will return. I ſhall not live to ſee it; you may." Cromwell ordered his funeral to be public, and gave two hundred pounds towards it. On his death-bed he told his friends, "It is a dangerous thing to leave every thing undone till our laſt illneſs. I fear a death-bed repentance will avail us little if we have lived vainly and viciouſly, and neglected our converſion till we can ſin no longer."

Uſher afforded this atteſtation to the merits of our excellent Liturgy:

"Of the Book of Common Prayer I have always had a reverent and a very high eſteem; and therefore that at any time I ſhould ſay it was an idol, is a ſhameleſs and a moſt abominable untruth.

"*Jan.* 16, 1655. J. ARMAGH."

The

The motto to his episcopal seal was, "*Ve mihi si non Evangelizarer*; wretched man that I am if I do not preach the Gospel." One of his directions to accomplish that salutary purpose is excellent: " Meddle with " controversies * and difficult points as little " as may be in your popular preaching; lest " you puzzle your hearers, or engage them in " wrangling disputations, and so hinder their " conversion, which is the main design of " preaching."

~~~~~

JUDGE HUTTON.

Echard says of this upright lawyer, "that " he was very conscientious and charitable, " and that he became conspicuous for giving " his judgment against ship-money; with " which the good King (Charles I.) was so " little disobliged that he still continued to " call him the honest judge."

* " Our clergy," says Dr. Butler, Bishop of Hereford, in one of his Charges, " are too apt in their discourses to " raise doubts against that religion they should merely teach; " they raise doubts to persons who have never heard them " before; and the doubts of those who have had the mis- " fortune to hear them before cannot be solved in a dis- " course of half an hour."

LORD

LORD KEEPER COVENTRY,

according to Echard, sent this request to his sovereign upon his death-bed, " that his Ma-
" jesty would take all distastes from the Par-
" liament summoned against next April (1639)
" with patience, and suffer it to sit without
" an unkind dissolution."

~~~~~

ELIZABETH STEPHENS.

" This young gentlewoman, of the age of
" sixteen, came to the Presence Chamber in
" 1648 to be touched for the evil, with which
" she was so afflicted that, by her own and
" her mother's testimony, she had not seen
" with her left eye for above a month.

" After prayers read by Dr. Sanderson, she
" knelt down to be touched with the rest
" by his Majesty. His Majesty then touched
" her in the usual manner, and put a ribbon
" with a piece of money hanging to it about
" her neck. Which done, his Majesty turned
" to the Duke of Richmond, the Earl of
" Southampton, and the Earl of Lindsey, to
" discourse with them. And the young gen-
" tlewoman

"tlewoman of her own accord said openly,
"'Now, God be praised! I can see of this
"sore eye;' and afterwards declared that she
"did see more and more by it, and could by
"degrees endure the light of the candle. All
"which his Majesty*, in the presence of the
"said Lords and many others, examined him-
"self and found to be true." OUDERT's
MS. Diary.

SERJEANT GLANVILLE,

SPEAKER OF THE HOUSE OF COMMONS,

being ordered by the House to put a question proposed to that assembly in 1628, replied, that he was otherwise commanded by the King. This brought up the learned Mr. Selden, who exclaimed, "Dare you "not, Mr. Speaker, put the question when "we command you? If you will not put

---

* The monarchs of France were supposed to possess this extraordinary power in descent from St. Louis. On the day after their coronation at Rheims they went in solemn procession to the abbey of St. Remy in that city, in the garden of which convent they touched all those afflicted with the evil that were brought to them, making the sign of the cross with their fingers upon the forehead of the diseased person, and exclaiming, "*Le Roi vous touche; Dieu "vous guerisse.*"

"it,

"it, we muſt ſit ſtill; thus we ſhall never
"be able to do any thing. They that come
"after you may ſay, 'We have the King's
"command not to do it.' We ſit here by the
"command of the King* under the great
"ſeal; and you are by his Majeſty, ſitting in
"his royal chair before both Houſes, ap-
"pointed for our Speaker; and now you
"refuſe to perform your office."

SIR JOHN BANKS, KNT.

ATTORNEY GENERAL TO CHARLES THE FIRST,

preſented an information in the Star Chamber in the eleventh year of that King's reign againſt divers perſons of quality for reſiding in London, contrary to a proclamation for that purpoſe in the eighth year of the reign of the ſame monarch.'

Amongſt other topics to enforce the obſervation of this order, he urges, that " by the

---

* A learned and acute Prelate of our times has incurred much obloquy for making uſe of words like theſe, words made uſe of by the moſt learned Engliſh lawyer that ever exiſted, by a lawyer whoſe motto was, " Liberty above all " things;" and the whole drift of whoſe conduct was to enforce liberty, not licentiouſneſs; for, as Tully nobly ſays, " *Libertas eſt poteſtas faciendi id quod jure licet*;" and where there is no law there can be no liberty.

" emigration

" emigration of the principal persons of Eng-
" land from their estates in the country to the
" metropolis, a great part of the money they
" drew from their tenants is exported far away
" from them, and is not issued into the parts
" from whence it ariseth, and that the people
" are not relieved therewith, or by their hospi-
" tality, or by being set to work by them; that
" they bring out of the country great numbers
" of idle and loose persons who follow them;
" that delinquents become so numerous, that
" the city and the places adjoining were not so
" easily governed by their magistrates as in for-
" mer times; that the people became diseased
" and infirm; that the provisions became dearer;
" that the country was left undefended; that the
" king, in imitation of his royal predecessors,
" had commanded the people, as well of the
" clergy as of the laity, to keep residence at
" their several dwellings in the several parts of
" the realm where, for defence and good safety
" thereof was most necessary; and to restrain
" their departure or changing their habitation
" from thence under divers pains; and that no-
" bleman or gentleman, bishop, rector, or cu-
" rate, unless he were in the service of the
" court or council, should, in forty days from
" the proclamation, depart from the city of
" London and Westminster, and the suburbs of
" them,

"them, and resort to their several counties
"where they usually reside, and there keep
"their habitations and hospitality, attend their
"services, and be ready for the defence and
"guidance of those parts as their callings,
"degrees, and abilities should extend."

The information then proceeds to specify the names of certain persons of rank, men and women, who have not paid obedience to the proclamation, and to request that they may be summoned to appear before the king in his Court of Star-Chamber.

HENRY MARTIN, ESQ.

having one day in the House of Commons made a long invective against Sir Harry Vane the elder, he continued, "But as for young "Sir Harry—" and sate down. Several persons cried out, "And pray what have you to "say to young Sir Harry?"—"Why, if young "Sir Harry lives long enough, he will be old Sir "Harry, that is all;" and then sate down again. Oliver Cromwell, one day in the House of Commons, called him in a scoffing manner Sir Henry Martin; Mr. Martin rises and bows

to Cromwell, adding, "I thank your *ma-
"jesty*; I always thought that when you were
"*king*, I should be knighted."

"I have lived," said he one day to Mr.
Speaker, "long enough to see the scripture
"saying fulfilled, ' Thou hast exalted the
"humble and meek; thou hast filled the
"hungry with good things, and the rich thou
"hast sent empty away*."

He was wont to sleep in the House. Alderman Atkins made a motion, that such scandalous members as slept, and did not attend to the business of the House, should be expelled. Martin starts up directly, and says, "Mr. Speaker, a motion has been just made to turn the nodders out of the House; I desire that the noddees may be included."

LORD CLARENDON.

The Earl of Rochester (Hyde) wrote the preface to the History, in which he was assisted

* Abbe Sieyes being one day asked, when he thought the French revolution would end said, "When a particular "part of the Magnificat is fulfilled;" those verses of it which Mr. Martin quoted.

by Dean Aldrich, who came often to Cornbury for that purpose, as well as for consulting his Lordship about the History. Lord Rochester appears always to have been extremely anxious that the History should be printed most scrupulously, as his father, Lord Clarendon, intended it.

"My Lord Clarendon (son of the Chancellor) told his Grace the Duke of Ormond, that the 'History of the Civil Wars' will make three volumes in folio; but it is probable that his Lordship may be mistaken in his calculation, and be too much governed by the bulk of it in the writing. The bishop of Rochester (Dr. Spratt), is desired to peruse, and to make some small corrections in the style, if any thing in it should appear to be amiss." *MS. Letter, Dr. Gibson to Dr. Charlett.*

The following passages are in one of the MS. copies of Lord Clarendon's History, and are not found in the printed copies. The figures shew the pages of the original from which they are taken.

MS. page 227, line 18 to 44.

"There was newly discovered a design amongst some citizens, with the privity of members

" members of both houses of best rank, to
" compel the Parliament by force to make
" peace with the King. The correspondence
" between the persons of honour and the
" citizens being managed by Mr. Waller;
" who, upon a slight discovery made by a
" false servant (who had overheard some dis-
" courses), very frankly confessed all he knew,
" and named lords, and ladies, and mer-
" chants; whereof some were condemned and
" executed, and others of all sorts impri-
" soned. The relation of that whole affair,
" and his miserable behaviour in it, deserve
" to be part of a more formal discourse. It was
" not thought proper to examine the business
" to the bottom when they found very conside-
" rable persons engaged or privy; but hav-
" ing taken the lives of some, with all the
" circumstances of terror, causing them to be
" executed in the streets before their own
" doors, in the sight of their neighbours
" (whereof one was a gentleman of good
" reputation, who had married a sister of
" Mr. Waller, and had been very assistant to
" him in his education, whom he sacrificed
" now without the least reluctancy), they
" thought it best to take the words of all the
" members of both Houses for their own in-
" demnity, by their severally pronouncing a
" solemn

" folemn proteftation, that they had no
" hand or privity in the defign and plot;
" and in which they promifed always to
" adhere to the Parliament, and to affift
" the forces raifed by Parliament againft the
" army raifed by the King (which was an ex-
" preffion never before heard of); and fo
" all jealoufies were extinguifhed; no man
" refufing or paufing to take it; chufing
" rather to run the hazard of it than to be
" made a fpectacle as his other friends were;
" though as foon as they had fecured them-
" felves by that facred vow, they made what
" hafte they could to the King for better
" fecurity, and where they might procure
" God's pardon as well as the King's without
" incurring any danger for afking it. Mr.
" Waller would have been glad to have got
" his own liberty at that price or any other;
" but he was kept in prifon, and continually
" threatened with death, which he feared
" and abhorred, till at laft he redeemed himfelf
" at a ranfom of ten thoufand pounds, to fupply
" the affairs of the Parliament, and as much
" more fpent upon divines and other inter-
" ceffors; befides marrying a wife whofe
" friends had contributed to his abfolution,
" and befides the difpofing them to do all
" this by a fpeech pronounced by him at the
" bar

" bar of the House of Commons of the great-
" est flattery and falsehood; such a mean-
" ness and lowness of spirit, that life itself
" was no recompence for it."

End of the Fifth Part.
MS. page 501, to the End.

" This declaration, as soon as printed, was
" sent over to Cologne, and the Chancellor
" was commanded by the King to write some
" discourse upon it to awaken the people,
" and to shew them their concernment in
" it; which he did by way of a letter to a
" friend, which was likewise sent into Eng-
" land, and there printed. When Cromwell
" called his next Parliament it was made
" great use of to inflame the people and make
" them sensible of the destruction that at-
" tended them, and was thought to produce
" many good effects; and so we conclude
" this part."

MS. page 411, line 28, to the End.

" All that passed at the Hague, both with
" the States and Scots, is more particularly
" contained in papers and memorials, but
" will be found in the Haire-Cabinet, out
" of

"of which any thing that is material may be
added or altered; as alfo the names of all
the minifters at the tyme in Madrid are in
a paper book that ftands in the fhopp."

Page 91, line 1 to line 19.

"His Majeftie's expedition to York, the
Earl of Strafford's going to the army, the
Earl of Northumberland remaining fick at
London, and the combination of the officers of the army againft him; the calling
the great court of the peers to attend his
Majefty, and the feveral intrigues there to
the prejudice of the King; the treaty at
Rippon, and the perfons employed in that
treaty; the petition fent from feveral of the
popular Lords to the King at York that he
would call a parliament; and the King's
refolution declared for iffuing writs to call
a Parliament at Weftminfter the third of
November following; the adjournment of
the treaty from Rippon to London, and
the engagement to pay 80,000l. per month
for the maintenance of the two armies,
with the fending the Earl of Pembroke,
with fome other Lords, to borrow 200,000
pounds of the city of London for the payment of the armies; the indirect and factious
contrivances

" contrivances to procure discontented per-
" sons to be chosen to serve in Parliament,
" and to prevent the election of those who
" were known to be well affected to the go-
" vernment; the artifices to incense the
" people against the government of the church
" and against the persons of the most eminent
" prelates; the notorious and seditious in-
" surrection of the seamen, and their attempt
" to take Lambeth House, the palace of the
" Archbishop of Canterbury, whom they at-
" tempted to murder; and many other extra-
" ordinary preparations towards the provoking
" and indisposing the ensuing Parliament, are
" particulars which cannot be omitted by any
" man whose business it will be to make a
" clear and lively representation of the temper
" and spirit of the times in the history of it.
" To the subject of this discourse little of it
" would be applicable; and it would be
" looked upon by exact surveyors as foreign
" to the matter."

P. 113, line 31 to line 36.

" The memorials and extracts are so large
" and particular of all these proceedings in
" the notes and papers of the person whose life *
" is at the end of this discourse, that even

* Lord Clarendon's.

" many

"many things are inserted not so immediately applicable to his own person, which
possibly may hereafter in some other method
be communicated to the world; and therefore we shall again resort only to such particulars as most immediately relate to him,
in which there will be sometimes a digres-
sion into foreign matters to make the other
understood."

Page 130, line 2 to line 6.

"It was at that time concluded that the
King chose rather to pass through the town
to Hampton Court, without staying at Whitehall, which many men wished he had done,
and which would have kept up the spirits
of his friends; and it was visible enough
the governing people feared it much, and
were dejected with the apprehension; but
in a few daies recovered their courage and
sent their remonstrance to the King by a
committee of their members to Hampton
Court; and at the same time sent it carefully over the kingdom in print and with
diligence," &c.

Page 503, line 4. *Government.*

"So that he might have enjoyed some part
"of that comfort and pleasure which Velleius
"Paterculus says Marius and Carthage had
"when his banishment reduced him to end
"his life in the ruins of that city, ' *Cum Ma-*
"*rius aspiciens Carthaginem, illa intuens Ma-*
"*rium alter alteri possent esse solatio;*' whilst he
"refreshed himself with the memory of his
"greatness when he overthrew the great and
"famous city, and she again delighted to
"behold her destroyer expelled from his
"country, which he had served so eminently,
"and forced, forsaken of all men, to end his
"life and to be buried in her ashes. If the
"King's nature could have been delighted
"with such reflection, he might have argu-
"ment abundant in seeing Scotland."

Page 558, ult.

"King's interest, and desiring well-affected
"men of all conditions, especially the city of
"London, to join with them, in order to the
"calling a free Parliament, for settling the
"government of the nation in church and
"state, with the determination whereof they
" would

" would willingly submit, and lay down their
" arms, with those expressions which they
" knew would be most acceptable to the
" Presbyterians, but giving all countenance,
" &c."

MS. page 560, line 34.

" discharged it well. It was a great blessing
" of God that this melancholy conjuncture
" happened in the winter, that men could not
" execute all the thoughts and purposes the
" unhappy state of affairs suggested to them.
" The King could not make his way by Ger-
" many till the spring; and in the mean time
" many men thought of providing a religion
" as well as other conveniences for the jour-
" ney, and that might be grateful to those
" people and places where they were like to
" reside. The Protestant religion was found to
" be very unagreeable to their fortune, and
" very many exercised their thoughts most
" how to get handsomely from it; and if it
" had not been for the King's own steadiness
" (which was very manifest) men would have
" been more out of countenance to have
" owned the faith they were of; and many
" made little doubt but that it would shortly
" be very manifest to the King, that his resto-
                             " ration

" ration depended wholly on Catholic princes,
" who would never be united but on behalf
" of the Catholic religion."

MSS. page 579, line 9.

" speech to him, in which he extolled the
" great service he had done to the Parliament,
" and therein to the kingdom, which was in
" danger to have lost all the liberty they had
" gotten with so vast an expence of blood and
" of treasure, and to be made slaves again,
" if he had not magnanimously declared him-
" self in their defence; the reputation whereof
" was enough to blast all their enemies de-
" signs, and to reduce all to their obedience.
" He told him that his memory should flourish
" to all eyes, and the Parliament (whose thanks
" he presented to him) would take all occa-
" sions to manifest their kindness and grati-
" tude for the service he had done. The
" General was not a man of eloquence or
" of any volubility of speech; he assured them
" of his constant fidelity, which should never
" be shaken, and that he would live and die
" in their service; and then informed them
" of the several addresses he had received in
" his march, and of the observation he made
" of the general temper of the people, and of
" their

"their *impatient desire of a free Parliament*, which
"he mentioned with more than his usual
"warmth, as a thing they would expect
"to be satisfied in *(which they observed and dis-*
"*liked)*; yet concluded, that having done his
"duty in this representation, and thereby
"complied with the promise he had made
"to those who had made their addresses, he
"entirely left the confideration and the de-
"termination of the whole to their wisdom;
"which gave them some ease and hopes that
"he could be faithful to them."

MSS. page 405, line 36.

"Here at Giron they found an old priest,
"who governed the town, and was master of
"the posts; an office which he had held when
"Lord Cottington was last there, when the
"Prince Charles the First was in Spain, who
"was a jolly talking man, and glad to hear
"old stories. They were no sooner in their
"lodging, but the Inquifition came to exa-
"mine the books they brought into the coun-
"try, at first with some rudeness, the chief of
"them being a priest of a large size, and a
"very barbarous aspect and behaviour. They
"urged to have a view of all the books they had,
"but afterwards were contented with the ca-
"talogue

"talogue of their names, subscribed by one
"of the secretaries; and received a piece of
"eight very thankfully.

"*Variations in* OLIVER CROMWELL'S CHA-
RACTER.

"To follow Machiavel's method" for
"totally declined Machiavel's method;" "was
"guilty of many crimes," for "had all the
"wickednesses;" for "virtues," "some good
"qualities;" for "brave bad man," "brave
"wicked man."

Memorandum, April 21st, 1756.

"This morning Dr. Terry, canon of Christ
"Church, came to see me; and knowing that
"he superintended the first edition of 'Lord
"Clarendon's History of the Rebellion,' and
"corrected the press, I asked him what be-
"came of the manuscript copy from which
"it was printed: he said, he thought it was
"returned to the Earl of Rochester. I men-
"tioned to him what I heard Sir Joseph Jekyll
"say lately in the House of Commons, that
"he had reason to believe, or to that purpose,
"that it was not printed faithfully. The
"Doctor assured me, that he knew of no one
"thing omitted, but an imperfect account
"of a bull feast at Madrid when the author
"was

" was ambassador there, which did not con-
" cern the purpose of the History; nor of any
" thing added, besides some circumstances of
" King Charles's removing from Brussels to
" Breda, which the Earl of Rochester de-
" clared he found in his father's papers. As
" for the rest, Dr. Terry assured me it was
" most exactly printed from the written copy,
" and the Earl of Rochester was so nicely
" scrupulous in having it followed, that he
" would not suffer any small variation, though
" only to make the sense clearer, and the com-
" position less intricate; which I have also
" heard confirmed by Dr. Aldrich, the late
" worthy dean of Christ Church, and my
" good friend Mr. Hill of Richmond, who
" both have been present when it was pro-
" posed to change or transpose a word or two,
" in order to make the sense and meaning of
" the author more perspicuous; and this pro-
" posal has sometimes been made by the Dean
" himself; but the Earl of Rochester would
" never consent to it, saying that it was his
" father's book, and should be printed as he
" left it, which his Lordship had solemnly
" promised when he received it.

" I asked Dr. Terry who wrote the pre-
" face to the first volume; he answered, the
"Earl

"Earl of Rochester he supposed; for it was
"delivered to him all in that Earl's hand, and
"printed from that copy.

"GEORGE CLARKE *."

Mr. Hyde, afterwards Lord Clarendon, was chairman of the Committee that sat upon the complaint made against the Earl Marshall's Court, as a court of honour, and delivered to the House of Commons the opinion of himself and of the Committee respecting it, "That "it had no jurisdiction to hold plea of words, "and that it was a grievance;" an opinion that must be universally adopted, when it is known that the following iniquitous decision was given by that Court:

"A citizen of London was complained of
"in this court, who, going to a gentleman
"well descended for some money that was
"due unto him, the gentleman not only
"refused to pay him the money, but gave
"him hard words; then said the citizen,
"Surely you are no gentleman that would not

---

* Extracted from the original in one of the blank leaves of Lord Clarendon's History, presented to the library of Worcester College, Oxford, by George Clarke, Esq. Secretary to Prince George of Denmark, and one of the Lords of the Admiralty.

" pay your debts*; with some other reflect-
" ing language, and the citizen underwent
" the censure of the court." RUSHWORTH.

Dom Noel D'Argonne, a Carthusian, of Gallion, in Normandy, says, " The Lord Chan-
" cellor (Clarendon) told me and his friends in
" that country, that the civil war in Charles
" the First's time took its rise from an opi-
" nion that was entertained, that the monarch
" intended to restore to the church the
" estates that had been taken from it at the
" time of the Reformation, and which had
" passed into the hands of the noblemen and
" principal gentlemen of England."

* A maxim has prevailed much in our time, that a man should be generous before he is just; as if a man could be truly generous before he is just. Justice, according to Aristotle, comprehending in itself every other virtue, the preference of one virtue to another, the sacrifice of that virtue we like least to another we like better, is a solecism in morality. Sterne says well in his ' Sermon upon Conscience,' " Trust not that man's conscience in one thing
" who has it not in every thing;" and words more awful inform us, that " he that is guilty of one breach of the
" commandments of God, is guilty of them all."

SAMUEL

SAMUEL BRET.

The Jews have in general been supposed to have proceeded in their traditions from father to son, without any of those public Councils which obtained so often in the Christian church. Samuel Bret gives an account of a Jewish Council, at which he was present, on the plain of Ageda, in Hungary, on the 12th of October 1650. The account of the matters agitated in it is very curious, and it ended *re infectâ*, as most Christian councils did. It is published in the fourth volume of ' The Phœnix,' in 1707; also at the end of Dr. Clayton, bishop of Clogher's ' Dissertation on Prophecy,' 8vo. 1749; and has lately been reprinted in a learned and elegant little work, entitled ' *Horæ Biblicæ*,' written by an eminent Advocate, who, to the profoundest and most extensive knowledge of his profession, adds a variety of erudition and literature hardly ever to be met with in the most finished scholar. To the detriment of the country and literature in general, the modesty of this elegant writer has permitted only a few copies of the work to be printed for the use of his friends. It is, however, most devoutly to be wished, that the great merit of the work may

prevail

prevail upon him to extend the diffusion of its valuable contents, and to give up his perſonal feelings to the wiſhes and inſtruction of the public.

The following letter on the ſubject of the 'Horæ Biblicæ' was received by the Compiler from an eminent Scholar in Scotland:

Edinburgh, 15*th Jan.* 1798.

"Dear Sir,

"I had the favour of your letter, and of
"what your friend has printed on the ſubject
"of the Bible and of the Jews, which I think
"is very well worth the reading. The Jews
"are certainly the moſt ancient people of
"whom we have any record; and their anti-
"quity is better vouched than that of any
"other people. Your friend has collected
"their Hiſtory ſince the taking of their city
"by the Romans, of which I was entirely
"ignorant till I read the book you ſent me.
"They are, I think, a moſt curious people
"in one reſpect; that they are a nation, and
"a moſt numerous nation, and very cloſely
"united, and yet they have no country pe-
"culiar to themſelves, but may be ſaid to be
"of I don't know how many countries. And
"in

" in this respect there is only one other race of
" men which I think can be compared to
" them, I mean the Gypsies. There are seve-
" ral very curious things mentioned in your
" friend's book; particularly the account he
" gives of the *Masorites*, who have furnished a
" specimen of such a reverential attention to
" the sacred books, and such a minute indus-
" try in executing not only all the verses, but
" all the words, and even all the letters of the
" twenty-four books of the Old Testament.
" This, I think, is the greatest curiosity of
" the literary kind that ever was heard of.
" He speaks of a butchery * of the Jews in
" the space of four years betwixt the years
" sixty-six and seventy of the Christian æra,
" when it is computed that two millions of
" them perished; I should be glad to know
" upon what occasion or for what cause. He
" gives us a very curious and interesting ac-
" count of a meeting of the Jews in the last
" century, where it was debated whether the
" Messiah was yet to come, or whether he
" was not already come, and whether Jesus
" Christ was not the Messiah. This inclines
" me to believe, that sooner or later the pro-

* This massacre of the Jews arose from their insurrec-
tions, and continual proneness to rebel against their governors.

" phecy

"phecy will be fulfilled of the Jews becoming Christians.

"I think of coming to London in the month of March next, if my health will permit, and taking my last leave of you and my other friends there. But if I should never see you again, be assured that I am most sensible of your friendship, and shall continue to the last hour of my life,

"Your Friend,
"And humble Servant,
"J. B.

"P. S. I am much obliged to you for making me the compliment which Solon made to himself, 'I grow old still learning.' I desire to live no longer than I am able to acquire knowledge, and can say with Solomon, 'That day unto day uttereth speech, and night unto night sheweth knowledge.'"

COUNTESS OF ORMONDE.

"It was my chance," says the learned Sir Thomas Smith, in one of his Orations on the proposed Marriage of Queen Elizabeth, "to
" be at dinner with the Countess of Ormonde,
" whom Sir Francis Benyon married. She
" said, she had now borne ten children, and
" that she was brought to bed not so nicely
" as the ladies are here in England, but either
" in a tent or a wide barn, after the manner of
" her country, Ireland: and I tell you,"
said she, " that I felt no manner of pain at
" these births; nor I see no cause why I
" should make so nice of the matter as you do
" here in England; we do not so in our
" country." Whereat an old lady was won-
" derfully offended, and said that they were
" beasts, and that Lady Ormonde was but a
" beast to say so. Then Lady Ormonde, as a
" witty lady, turned the matter, and said it
" was a gift which St. Patrick begged of Our
" Lady for his countrywomen. But the
" truth is," adds Sir Thomas, " that all wo-
" men do not stir about to travail and to labour
" as they do there, where they do not use them-
" selves to rest and to ease; as they can better
" away with travail because of use, so they
" bear

"bear that travail of childbirth with much more ease, or in manner without pain."—
Sir Thomas Smith's Life, 8vo. 1718.

INIGO JONES.

"January 18, 1635.

"The last month, the queen's (Henrietta Maria's) chapel in Somerset House was consecrated by her bishop. The ceremony lasted three days; massing, preaching, and saying of litanies. Such a splendid scene built over the altar, *the Glory of Heaven!* Inigo* Jones never presented a more cu-

---

* The genius of this great architect for ornament did not sink below the invention of Milton and the learning of Ben Jonson, whose masques he embellished with every grace and propriety of scenical decoration. He built the Queen's Chapel at Whitehall, one of the most happy efforts of his architectural talents, and which has given rise to the present elegant front of Somerset House, more decorated indeed than the original, but in which, as the architect of it always said, he did not stir any step without consulting those two great masters of his, Palladio and Scamozzi. The screen of the Queen's Chapel, by Jones, was made a green-house by Sir William Chambers for his garden at Whitton near Hounslow, and in that state exhibits all the purity of ornament, and grandeur of effect, for which this master was so deservedly celebrated. In the opinion of one of the French translators of Vitruvius, the Banqueting House at Whitehall is the finest specimen of architecture on this side of the Alps.

rious

"rious piece in any of the mafques at White-
" hall."—*Mr. Gerard to Lord Strafford.*

JOHN MILTON.

In fpite of the virulence of party, Echard thus defcribes this great writer: " He was " the wonder of the age! Though always " affecting uncommon and heterodox opi- " nions: Latin fecretary firft to the parlia- " ment, and afterwards to Oliver Cromwell; " and a moft inveterate enemy to King Charles. " But what did moft, and moft juftly, diftin- " guifh him, was his poetry, particularly his " ' Paradife Loft,' in which he manifefts fuch a " wonderful and fublime genius as was never " exceeded in any age or nation, and of " which it appears impoffible to give foreign " nations any idea." It feems indeed re- ferved to our times to break through the fpell, and to give to every country in the world an adequate notion, not only of the fubli- mity but of the beauty of Milton's genius. Mr. Fufeli's pencil, equally fuccefsful in ex- preffing ideas of amenity as of grandeur, is the only true tranflator this great poet has ever poffeffed. The languages of other countries indeed fink under the grand and beautiful

images

images of Milton; but, like Michael Angelo's, the commentator of the terrible and gigantic ideas of Dante in the Seftine Chapel, Fuſeli's pencil will pourtray the evaneſcent images of our divine bard, and give an habitation and a ſhape to his ideal forms, which the prints to be made from his paintings will diſplay wherever there ſhall be eyes to behold them.

It had been reported, that James the Second, when Duke of York, ſaid, "That the blindneſs of Milton was a judgment of heaven upon him for his daring impiety in writing againſt his father Charles the Firſt."—"Be it ſo, then," replied Milton; "but what was the execution of the Duke's father upon a public ſcaffold * ?"

SIR BULSTRODE WHITELOCK.

WHEN a meeting was held at the Speaker's houſe by the Lord General Cromwell and the other officers of the army and ſtate, reſpecting the ſettlement of the kingdom after the death of Charles the Firſt, this great lawyer obſerved, that

* Horace ſays wiſely,
—————— *Quid æternis minorem*
Conſiliis animum fatigas?

"The laws of England were so interwoven with
"the power and practice of monarchy, that to
"settle a government without something of
"monarchy in it would make so great an alte-
"ration in the proceedings of the law, that
"they had scarce time to rectify it, nor could
"they well foresee the inconveniences that
"would arise thereby; therefore, he insisted,
"that there might be a day given for the late
"king's eldest son, or for the Duke of York
"his brother, to come in to the parliament;
"and, upon such terms as should be fit and
"agreeable both to our civil and spiritual
"liberties, a settlement might be made with
"them*."

LORD LEICESTER.

"In the year 1639," says his Lordship in
his Journal, "King Charles sent for me to
"come out of France (at the beginning of
"our unhappy wars and differences with the
"Scots); I was then in great favour at court,
"and the king commanded me to follow him
"to York, which I did; but it was not
"God's will that the king should follow the
"advice which I gave him, to accommodate

* A similar sentiment took place in the mind of the great Lord Chatham, nearly at the end of the late disastrous American war.

"his

"his differences with the Scots, and not to make war where nothing was to be gained, and much might be loft, which the world hath fince feen to be true."

Of the minifters of Louis XIII. king of France, he fays, "If I can guefs at all at them, they muft be plainly and roundly dealt with. I know they are full of tricks, which makes them look for the like in others; but I tell them the king my mafter will not be fed with tricks; and therefore they muft come off freely and fully with what they mean to do, and not deliver it by piecemeal."

CHARLES THE SECOND,
KING OF ENGLAND.

"I was told," fays the Earl of Dartmouth, "by one that was converfant with this prince, that he had a conftant maxim, which was, never to fall out with any one, let the provocation be ever fo great; by which, he said, he had found great benefit all his life; and the reafon he gave for it was, that he did not know how foon it might be necef-
"fary

"fary for him to have them again for his beft
"friends."

LORD ROCHESTER.

Could any thing render vice more defpicable than it really is in itfelf, it would be the behaviour of this diffipated peer on his deathbed. According to Aubrey, at that dreadful period he fent for all his fervants (not excepting his cowherd) up to his bedfide, and made a folemn recantation of his former life and opinions.

He ufed (according to the fame writer) to fay of himfelf, " that whilft he remained in " the country, he did tolerably well; but " that as foon as he came to Brentford, he " felt the devil enter into him."

During his laft illnefs he often exclaimed, " Mr. Hobbes and the philofophers have been " my ruin:" then putting his hand upon a large bible that lay befide him, he cried out with great rapture, " This, this, is the " true philofophy."

ALGERNON.

ALGERNON SYDNEY.

This extraordinary man thus deſcribes to his father his ſituation when he was living in exile upon the Continent. The Letter is dated from Freſcati, near Rome, 1661.

"Here is what I look for, health, quiet, and ſolitude. I am with ſomme eagerneſſe fallen to reading, and finde ſoe much ſatisfaction in it, that though I every morning ſee the ſunne riſe, I never goe abroade 'till ſix or ſeven of the clock at night. Yet cannot I be ſoe ſure of my temper as to know certainly how long this manner of life will pleaſe me. I cannot but rejoice, and am delighted to find, that when I wander as a vagabonde through the world, forſaken of my friends, poore and known only to be a broken limbe of a ſhip-wrecked faction, yet I find humanity and civility from thoſe who are in the height of fortune and reputation. But I doe alſoe well know I am in a ſtrange land, how far thoſe civilities do extend, and that they are too aery to feed or clothe a man. I cannot ſo unite my thoughts unto one object as abſolutely to forbid the memory of ſuch things as

"as these are to enter into them, but I go as
"farre as I can; and since I cannot forget
"what has passed, nor be absolutely insensible
"of what is present, I defend myself reason-
"ably well from increasing or anticipating
"evils by foresight. The power of foresee-
"ing is a happy quality unto those who
"prosper, and can ever propose to themselves
"something of greater felicity than they
"enjoy; but a most desperate mischief to
"them who by foreseeing can discover no-
"thing that is not worse than the evils which
"they do already feele: he that is naked,
"alone, and without help, in the open sea, is
"lesse unhappy in the night, when he may
"hope the land is near, than in the day when
"he sees it not, and that there is no possibi-
"lity of safety."

WILLIAM PRYNNE.

Mr. Gerard says, in one of his letters to Lord Strafford, " No mercy shewed to
" Prynne. He stood in the pillory, and
" lost his first ear in a pillory in the palace
" of Westminster, in full term; his other in
" Cheapside; where whilst he stood his vo-
" lumes were burnt under his nose, which
" had almost suffocated him.
" Prynne,

"Prynne, prisoner in the Tower, is re-lapsed into new errors; he hath got his ears cured, so that they grow again."

Gerard to Lord Strafford.

Prynne at the Restoration became a zealous royalist, and served on a commission of array for Charles the Second at Bath. He was so voluminous a writer, that the late Sir William Blackstone, who was anxious to possess all his tracts, could never satisfy himself that he had made a complete collection of them.

JAMES THE SECOND,
KING OF ENGLAND.

In the ci-devant church of the English Benedictines at Paris was deposited the body of this ill-advised monarch, with the following inscription ordered by himself:

Cy gyst
Jacques II.
Roi de la Grande Bretagne.

His body has most probably suffered that outrage which the modern French have in general so liberally bestowed upon the bodies of sovereigns.

reigns. His MS. papers, and the Memoirs of his own Life, written by Himself, likewife in MS. have very probably suffered the fame fate with that of the body of him who wrote them.

" Church* and King are the fame thing; " they ftand or fall together," faid this prince to

* Heads of a Petition to the Parliament in Charles the Firſt's Time.

" We become fuitors for the continuance of thofe pious
" foundations of cathedral churches, which with their lands
" and revenues were dedicated to the fervice of God, foon
" after the plantation of chriftianity in this kingdom.

* * * *

" As approved and confirmed by the laws of the land,
" ancient and modern.

" As the principal eventual motive and encouragement of
" all ftudents, efpecially in divinity.

" As affording a competent portion in an ingenuous
" way to many younger brothers of good parentage, who
" devote themfelves to the miniftry of the gofpel.

* * * *

" As the goodly monuments of our predeceffors piety,
" and the prefent honour of this kingdom in the eye of
" foreign nations †.

" As the chief fupport of many thoufand families of the
" laity, who enjoy fair eftates from them in a free way."

† " England," fays Sir William Chambers, " is rich in
" the fplendor of her ancient ftructures, and contains many
" mag-

to the vice-chancellor of Oxford the last time he visited that university. This observation the rash and deluded sovereign found to be true in his own country; and in a neighbouring one we have seen it again verified. The nobility and the third estate in France joined against the clergy, in hopes to share in the spoils of that venerable order, and in destroying it destroyed themselves, and their sovereign with them. The same right which the two orders had to their possessions sanctioned by law itself, the clergy had to their's; and one violation of justice in a state, like the interstice made of old in the Macedonian legion, effects the destruction of the whole.

Omne in præcipiti vitium stetit;

and he must be a short-sighted politician indeed, who does not see that, when once the ideas of mankind are confounded on subjects

---

" magnificent examples of Gothic architecture, equally ad-
" mirable for the art with which they are built, and the taste
" and ingenuity with which they are composed." Sensible of
of these advantages, our present Deans and Chapters, with a
pious and elegant care, attend strenuously to the preservation
and support of the sacred structures committed to their charge;
and, under the direction of that ingenious architect Mr.
James Wyatt, bestow upon them beauties unknown to
those who built them, and add to vastness and to grandeur
the magic of perspective, and the charms of picturesque
decoration.

which

which they have ever held facred and venerable, and when want of principle, and a general carelefsnefs refpecting right and wrong, take place, property, the creature of eftablifhed government, invaded in one inftance, will lead to the invafion of itfelf in every other; and thofe who counfelled its firft violation will not be the laft to feel the effects of their own pernicious doctrines in what themfelves may poffefs.

"It was the practice of this prince," fays Mr. Nairne, " ever fince he firft appeared in " the world, to write fhort notes from time to " time of all that was remarkable in the af- " fairs wherein he had any fhare. All thofe " memoirs of paffages which occurred before " his laft efcape out of England have been " happily preferved, though they were written " on feveral loofe papers; they have been " fafely kept by his own order in the library " of the Scotch College at Paris *."

James

* It is to be hoped that care has been taken of thefe papers in the French Revolution, as well as of many other very curious ones relative to the tranfactions of King James the Second's reign and the archbifhoprick of Glafgow, which were depofited in the fame place. Could they poffibly find their way to that excellent repofitory of curious MSS. the Britifh Mufeum, it would furely be well worth the attention

James the Second lays in the account of his life written by himself:

" 1695. The king applies himself wholly to devotion, and makes a journey to La Trappe." He adds, " I am a great admirer of La Trappe, and of the holy and exemplary lives of the monks in that convent, and am overjoyed when I hear that any person has left the world to retire thither."

King James's frequent pilgrimages to La Trappe are often mentioned in the Letters of Lord Middleton and Secretary Caryll. He kept up a constant correspondence with the celebrated M. de Rancé, abbot of that convent, who introduced into it a more rigid and austere discipline than that to which its monks had been accustomed *.

of parliament to secure these authentic records in that kingdom, the history of which they would so forcibly illustrate. They might, not long since, have been purchased for two thousand pounds.

* By the piety and benevolence of Mr. Weld, the monks of this venerable order, fugitives from the persecution and impiety of the government of France, have found an asylum in this country, which they enjoy in the beautiful and peaceable shades of Lulworth Castle.

JOHN HOUGH
BISHOP OF WORCESTER

JOHN HOUGH, D. D.

LORD BISHOP OF WORCESTER.

The Engraving of this excellent Prelate was made from an original drawing by Mr. Richardſon, and well exhibits the character of the Biſhop's mind, ſpirit, and ſweetneſs of difpoſition. The exhibition of one part of his character, his manly and dignified behaviour reſpecting the arbitrary conduct of James the Second and his unprincipled miniſtry at Magdalen College, Oxon, can never be forgotten by his admiring and grateful countrymen, as long as they preſerve the leaſt regard for the real liberties of their favoured country; and his milder virtues will long be remembered in the placid vale of Hartlebury, where his charity to the poor, his friendlineſs to his neighbours, and the elegant and cheerful ſimplicity of his difpoſition, have ſtill left behind them indelible traces in the memories of many perſons.

The following letter of Dr. Hough is printed in Mr. Green's excellent 'Hiſtory of Worceſter,' and has been ſuppoſed the laſt he ever wrote. It was addreſſed by the Biſhop, three weeks before his death, to Lord Digby:

" My

" My Lord,   *April* 13, 1743.

"I think myself much obliged to your Lordship's nephew for his kind visit, whereby I have a more authentic account of your Lordship's health than is usually brought me by report, and an opportunity of informing myself in many particulars respecting your noble house, and the good family; of which I hear with uncommon pleasure by one who hath been no stranger to them."

"The young gentleman will account to your Lordship for Hartlebury; but I fancy you will expect me to say something of myself, and therefore I presume to tell you my hearing hath long failed. I am weak and forgetful; having as little inclination to business as ability to perform it. In other respects I have ease (which may be more properly called indolence) to a degree beyond what I durst have thought on when years began to multiply upon me. I wait continually for a deliverance out of this world into a better, in humble confidence that by the mercy of God, through the merits of his Son, I shall stand at the resurrection at his right hand. And when you, my Lord, have ended those days that are to come (which I pray may be many and prosperous)

"perous) as innocently and as exemplarily as
"thofe that are paſt, I doubt not of our
"meeting in that ſtate where the joys are
"renewable and will always endure.

"I am your Lordſhip's

"Moſt obedient and affectionate ſervant,

"Jo. WORCESTER."

This worthy prelate, whom his friend and neighbour, Lord Lyttleton, fays in his 'Perfian Letters' "no one ever thought lived too long, "unlefs it was out of an impatience to fucceed "him," died, univerſally beloved and lamented. May 8, 1743, in the ninety-third year of his age, and was buried in the cathedral of Worceſter. The monument dedicated to his memory is the maſter-piece of the genius of Roubiliac. The bas-relief upon it reprefents the Biſhop before the Privy Council of James the Second, where he behaved with that manly yet placid firmnefs which ſhewed that it was regard to his duty and his fituation alone that made him oppofe the violent and arbitrary meaſures of the executive government. The figure of the Biſhop is very grand; he appears to be in a pious extafy, his countenance beaming with tranfport, with his hands claſped together, and his eyes uplifted to Heaven,

Heaven, as if anticipating those beatitudes which are promised to all those whose lives, like his, shall be distinguished by worthy and by virtuous energies, by the most active benevolence and by the most ardent piety.

Bishop Hough sent the following circular letter to the clergy of his diocess on occasion of a dreadful fire that happened at Wellingborough. It breathes the same spirit of charity and simplicity that pervaded every thing this good prelate did:

" GOOD BROTHER,
" You have heard some time since of the
' dismal calamity that befel the inhabitants
" of Wellingborough, in the county of Nor-
" thampton, by fire. It was dreadful in every
" circumstance, and I doubt not but you ten-
" derly sympathized with the sufferers. They
" now apply to your compassion for relief.
" Their deplorable case pleads strongly for it;
" and you, I am sure, will exert yourselves in
" stirring up the charitable dispositions of your
" people.

" Universal love, especially to those who
" are of the household of faith, and particularly
" to such as groan under heavy affliction, is
" the

" the distinguishing character of a Christian.
" It is the root of Christianity, and is the surest
" evidence of sincerity in the professors of it.
" I therefore most earnestly recommend to
" you this labour of love; and, praying God
" to bless and prosper you in all your cares
" for the service of the church,

 " I remain, good Brother,

  " Your very affectionate Brother,

   " Jo. Worcester."

The following anecdote of Bishop Hough's good-humour is told upon respectable authority: " He kept a very hospitable table, and was
" visited by all the gentry of his neighbour-
" hood. A whimsical lady in a certain situa-
" tion, with her husband, dining with him,
" was much pleased with a silver turenne
" which she saw at his table; and on her going
" home was, or pretended to be, ill in conse-
" quence of the extreme desire she had for it.
" Remonstrances, entreaties were in vain, and
" the poor husband for quiet's sake was ob-
" liged to go to the Bishop and tell him the si-
" tuation of his wife. The Bishop gave him
" the turenne for his lady; and some time af-
" terwards, when the lady had produced a
" chopping boy and was out of her bed, the
      " Bishop

"bishop sent a note to her to congratulate her on her safe delivery; and to say, that he now in his turn longed for the turenne, which, however, should be always at her service whenever she again longed for it."

BISHOP BURNET,

while he was one day preaching before the House of Commons at St. Margaret's church, turned his hour glass to shew that he was to continue his discourse; and was nearly interrupted by the applauding murmurs of his hearers.

The prejudice and the rascality of party has attempted to traduce this excellent prelate's character. He appears to have been a man of true piety and virtue, though occasionally a slave to his credulity. When in residence at his see of Salisbury, he preached every Thursday night in St. Thomas's church in that city. What can be conceived more impressive and more solemn than the conclusion of his History? what stronger arguments can be used in favour of religion, of virtue, and of patriotism, than those he has there made use of? and his appeal to the consciences of his readers

readers is one of the moſt ſtriking and ſolemn paſſages we have in our language. It was printed ſeparately in 12mo. in 1751, by Mr. Millar, and in theſe times of laxity of principle, and of fluctuation of opinion reſpecting government, it ſhould be again preſented to the notice of the public.

" Gaming," ſays the biſhop in this addreſs,
" is a waſte of time, riſing out of idleneſs,
" and kept up by covetouſneſs. The ill me-
" thods of ſchools and colleges give the chief
" riſe to the irregularities of our gentry, as
" the breeding young women to vanity, dreſſ-
" ing, and a falſe appearance of wit and be-
" haviour, without proper work, or a due
" meaſure of knowledge, and a ſerious ſenſe
" of religion, is the ſource of the corruption
" of that ſex. Something like *monaſteries with-*
" *out vows* would be a glorious * deſign, and
" might be ſo ſet on foot as to be the honour
" of a queen on the throne."

* So thought that great and good politician, Cardinal Ximenes, the ſenſible and wily Madame Maintenon, and the acute Catharine the Second, Empreſs of Ruſſia. See the excellent and entertaining account of her life and hiſtory, publiſhed by the Rev. Mr. Tooke, late Chaplain to the Britiſh Factory at Peterſburgh, 3 vols. 8vo.

" True

"True religion," concludes the bishop, "is the perfection of human nature, and the joy and delight of every one that feels it strong and active within. It is true, that it is not attained all at once; and it will have an unhappy allay even about a good man; but as those ill mixtures are the perpetual grief of his soul, so it is his chief care to watch over, and to mortify them. He will be in a continual progress, still gaining ground upon himself; and as he attains to a greater degree of purity, he will find a noble store of life and of joy growing upon him. Of this I write with the more concern and emotion, because I have felt this the true, and indeed the only joy which runs through a man's heart and life. It is that which has been for many years my greatest support. I feel from it the earnest of that supreme joy which I pant and long for. I am sure that there is nothing else which can afford any true or complete happiness. I have (considering my sphere) seen a great deal of all that is most shining and tempting in this world. The pleasures of sense I did soon nauseate. Intrigues of state, and the conduct of affairs, have something in them which is more specious, and I was for some years deeply immersed in them; "but

" but still with hopes of reforming the world,
" and of making mankind wiser and better;
" but I have found " *that which is crooked*
" *cannot be made straight.*" I acquainted my-
" self with knowledge and learning, and that
" in a great variety, and with more compass
" than depth; but though *wisdom excelleth folly,*
" *as much as* light doth darkness, yet it is a
" *sore trial*; for it is so very defective, that
" what is wanting to complete it, *cannot be*
" *numbered.* I have seen that *two were better*
" *than one,* and *that a threefold cord is not easily*
" *loosed*; and I have therefore cultivated friend-
" ship with much zeal, and a disinterested
" tenderness; but I have also found that was
" also vanity and vexation of spirit, though it
" be of the best and noblest sort. So that, up-
" on great and long experience, I could en-
" large upon the preacher's text, ' Vanity of
" vanities, all is vanity;' and I must also
" conclude with him, ' *Fear God and keep his*
" *commandments, for this is the end of man*;' the
" whole both of his duty and his happiness."

Indeed, the whole of this address may, excepting a few political notions not applicable
to these times, be perused with great improvement by all those, who wish to see the
advantages of a peaceful government, of excellent morality, and of a proper sense of religion,

ligion, pourtrayed in the strongest and most vivid colours.

WILLIAM THE THIRD.

The great work which this illustrious prince came to England to effect, Bishop Hurd thus eloquently and elegantly describes:

" The Revolution will be considered by
" grateful posterity as the true æra of Eng-
" lish liberty. It was interwoven, indeed,
" with the very principles of the constitu-
" tion. It was inclosed in the ancient trunk of
" the feudal law, and was propagated from it;
" but the operation was weak and partial in
" that state of its infancy. It acquired fresh
" force and vigour with age, and has now at
" length extended its influence to every part
" of the political system.

" Soon, however, after our liberation from
" a gloomy and bloody tyrant, the nation
" appeared to forget its deliverer; ingra-
" titude and vexation embittered the remain-
" der of his just and glorious reign, and caused
" him in a moment of just indignation to ex-
" claim,

" claim, ' Had I a fon, by heaven they would
" not have dared to ufe me fo."

The ill-treatment this fovereign, the wifeft and the moſt acute that has ever reigned over theſe kingdoms, met with from the country that was firſt fo much indebted to him, extorted theſe reflections from his enemy and his adverſary, the depoſed James the Second.

1698.
" The Prince of Orange ill-treated by his
" parliament. They tore his laurels from
" *his* brows, and placed them on their own.
" They made him account like a fteward for
" all the money they put into his hands.
" They forced him to fend away his Dutch
" troops, though he humbled fo far as to fend
" a letter by way of petition to the Houſe of
" Commons." *James the Second's Diary.*

On giving the character of King William,
" We quit him with reluctance," fays Sir J.
" Dalrymple. " There was a fimplicity, an
" elevation, and an utility in all the actions of
" his life."

QUEEN

QUEEN MARY.

" The Duke of Leeds told me, that King
" William before he went abroad told him,
" that he muſt be very cautious of ſaying any
" thing before the Queen that looked like diſ-
" reſpect to her father, which ſhe never for-
" gave any body, and that the Marquis of
" Halifax in particular had loſt all manner
" of credit with her for ſome unſeaſonable
" jeſts he had made upon this ſubject. The
" Earl of Nottingham, who was much in her
" confidence, told me, he was very ſure if
" ſhe outlived her huſband, ſhe would have
" done her utmoſt to have reſtored her father,
" but under ſuch reſtrictions as ſhould have
" prevented his ever making any attempt
" upon the religion or the liberty of his
" country." *MS. Letters.*

" Queen Mary's letters are models of ſim-
" plicity and affection. She ſays in one of
" them to her illuſtrious huſband, ' I always
" write what I think ;' and indeed her words
" and her actions ſeem to agree. This ex-
" cellent princeſs was placed in a difficult
" ſituation, between her affection to her fa-
                                    " ther,

"ther, and her duty to her hufband, in con-
"formity to the precept of the founder of her
"holy religion, fhe preferred the latter to
"the former.

"Queen Mary was once requefted to par-
"don a houfe-breaker, whilft her hufband was
"in Ireland. She wifely denied the requeft,
"and gave as a reafon, that King William
"would never pardon an offence of fo infi-
"dious and fo pernicious a nature, an offence
"that ftrikes at domeftic fecurity itfelf.

"Queen Mary has all the fubmiffion of a
"good wife, who leaves all to the direction
"of the king, and diverts herfelf with walk-
"ing fix or feven miles a day, and looking
"after her buildings, making of fringes, and
"fuch like innocent things; and does not
"meddle in government, though fhe has bet-
"ter title to do it, than the late Queen had."
Letter of Finch, Earl of Nottingham.

It was obferved by one of the perfons
who attended the addrefs of condolence
from the Univerfity of Oxford, on the death
of Queen Mary, that King William's eyes
filled with tears two or three times as they
were delivering that memorial of her virtues,
and of his affliction."

LORD

LORD DUNDEE.

"If terror ended or prevented war," said this intrepid nobleman, "it were true mercy." "The severity of his discipline," says Sir J. Dalrymple, "was dreadful. The only pu-
"nishment he inflicted upon his troops was
"death. "All other punishment," said he,
"disgraces a gentleman, and all that I have
"with me are of that rank. Death is a re-
"lief from the consciousness of crime."
"It is reported of him, that having seen a
"youth fly in his first action, he pretended
"that he had sent him to the rear on a mes-
"sage. The youth fled a second time: he
"brought him to the front of the army and
"shot him through the head with a pistol,
"observing, "That a gentleman's son ought
"not to fall by the hands of the hangman *."

That elegant Latin poet, Dr. Pitcairne, wrote the following beautiful lines, as an epitaph for Lord Dundee:

---

* Aristotle says in his "Politics," that stripes and blows have often proved fatal to the lives of kings and persons in power. Archelaiis, the tyrant of Macedon, was killed at the instigation of Decamnichus, whom he had caused to be scourged. See Dr. Gillis's excellent translation of Aristotle, vol. ii. p. 368.

Ultimo

Ultime Scotorum, potuit quo sospite solo
Libertas patriæ silva fuisse tuæ
Te moriente, novos accepit Scotia Reges
Accepitque novos te moriente Deos.
Illa tibi superesse negat, tu non potes illi,
Ergo Calidoniæ nomen inane vale
Tuque vale gentis priscæ fortissime Ductor
Optime Scotorum, atque optime Græme vale.

O laſt of Scots, whoſe life alone could ſtay
Thy country's freedom 'gainſt a foreign ſway!
See how thy death her every woe ſupplies,
New tyrants threaten, and new altars riſe.
Thy hapleſs lot involves ſad Scotia's fate,
Bereft of all that once had made her great.
Farewell, brave leader of thy country's fires,
Graham's bright name itſelf with thee expires!

Lord Dundee thus addreſſed his troops previous to the fatal battle of Killicranky.

" You are come hither this day to fight,
" and that in the beſt of cauſes; for it is
" the battle of your king, your religion, and
" your country, againſt the fouleſt uſurpation
" and rebellion. Having, therefore, ſo great
" a cauſe in your hands, I doubt not but it
" will inſpire you with an equal courage to
" maintain it; for there is no proportion be-
" tween treaſon and loyalty, nor ſhould there
" be any betwixt the valour of good ſubjects
" and traitors. Remember that to-day be-
" gins the fate of your king, your religion,
" and

"and your country. Behave yourselves, there-
"fore, like true Scotchmen, and let us by
"this action redeem the credit of this nation,
"that is laid low by the mischances and cow-
"ardice of some of our countrymen, in which
"I ask nothing of you that you shall not see
"me do before you. And if any of us shall
"fall on this occasion, we shall have the ho-
"nour of dying in our duty, and as becomes
"true men of valour and of conscience; and
"such of us as shall live and win the battle,
"shall have the reward of a gracious king,
"and the praise of all good men. In God's
"name then let us go on, and let this be your
"word, King James and the Church of Scot-
"land, which God long preserve."

Soon after this engagement, King William asked if Lord Dundee was not at Edinburgh, and was answered in the negative. "Then," said he, "I am sure he cannot be "alive." He was indeed killed in the battle of Killicranky.

SIR CHARLES LITTLETON, BART.

was Brigadier General to King James the Second. On making his apology to him, for his

sons

sons going off to King William, James replied, " Alas, Sir, are not my daughters with " him?"

After the revolution, King William offered to Sir Charles to send him Major General to Flanders, and to give him a regiment to fight against the French, of whose growing power Sir Charles was known to be apprehensive. He replied, " I cannot, Sir, accept of your " very gracious offer. I have great obligations " to my old master King James; I hear that he " will be in the French camp; and if he should " be there, I should not answer but that I " may desert to him."—" Sir Charles," says William nobly, " you are a man of honour. " I will not desire you to act against your " principles. Disturb not the government, " and I am sure we shall be very good friends."

JOHN SELDEN.

This learned man, the glory of the English nation according to Grotius, thus describes his countrymen:

" The

"The people are of a middle temper, according to their climate; the northern melancholy, and fouthern choler, meeting in their general conſtitution, doth render them ingenious and active; which, nouriſhed alfo under the wings of liberty, infpires a courage generous, and not foon out of breath. Active they are; and fo nigh to pure act, that nothing hurts them more than pure quiet.

* * * *

"Their ingenuity will not allow them to be excellent at the cheat, but they are rather fubject in that kind to take than to give; and, fuppofing others as open hearted as themſelves, are many times in treaties overmatched by thofe whom they overmatch in arms. Upon the fame account, they are neither ungenerous over thofe that are beneath, nor ſtubborn againſt them that are above them. Man, woman, or child, is all one with them, they will honour majefty wherever they fee it, and of the twain, tender it more when they fee it fet upon infirmity, as if they knew how to command themſelves only in order to the public good.

"Neverthelefs,

"Nevertheless, they love much *to be free* *.
"When they were under awe of the Pope's
"curse, they bore off designs by the head
"and shoulders, but afterwards by watchful-
"ness and foresight: and, having attained a
"light in religion that will own their liber-
"ties, of them both they made up one gar-
"land, not to be touched by any rude hand;
"but as if it were the bird of the eye, the
"whole body startles therewith, the alarm is
"soon given and taken, and when the alarm
"is given, neither high nor low are spared
"that stand in their way.

"This they do owe to the Eastern people,
"from whom they fetch their pedigree. So

---

* "*Liberty above all things*," was the motto of this learned and excellent man; not that abstract liberty, the notion of which, at present, threatens the destruction of every government in Europe; but that tempered and useful liberty, for which Selden exerted himself with great spirit and energy; that liberty which secures to every individual the blessings of personal safety and private property, under the sanction of law,— and which is more generally enjoyed in this nation, than it has ever been in any other country in the world.

† "*I would fain see that Blessed form*," says Tully; and in a true spirit of the indisputable maxim, the republics of Lacedæmon, however the great door of it profession, taken together, I chuse to shew that real law is necessary to insure true liberty, and that where there is no law, there can be no liberty.

"the only way to conquer them is to let them
have their liberties; for, like some horses,
they are good for carriage as long as their
burdens are easy, and set loose upon them;
but if too close girt, they will break all,
or cast their load and die.

* * *

"The two states of Lords and Commons,
in their transinigration, being then in the
nature of an army of soldiers, had a General
by their election under whom, after they
had obtained a peaceable settling, they
named anew by the name of Konning (or
the wise man), for then wisdom was more
necessary than valour. But after the clergy
had won the day, and this Konning had
submitted himself to the ghostly father, they
baptized him by the new name of Rex, and
so he is styled on all written monuments
which we owe entirely to ecclesiastics, although the vulgar held their appellation still,
which by construction, or rather corruption,
did at length arrive at the word *King*, a notion which as often changeth the sense as
the air, some making the persons all in all,
and some nothing at all, but a compliment
of state.

Speaking of the alteration made in the condition of the House of Commons of England, by Henry the Seventh, he concludes, " Henceforth the Commons of England are " no mean persons, and their representatives " of such concernment, as if a king will have " them to observe him, he must serve them " with their liberties and laws, and every one " the public good of the people. No man's " work is beneath, no man's above it. The " best honour of the king's work is to be *nobilis* " *servitus* (as Antigonus said to his son), or in " plain English, *supreme service* above all. I " now conclude, wishing we may obtain the " happiness of our fore-fathers, the ancient " Saxons, who, according to Tacitus, were " *quilibet sorte propriâ contentus*," every one " contented with his own situation. *Discourses on the Laws and Government of England, &c.*

~~~~~~

LORD TREASURER OXFORD,

in speaking of the different factions of Whig and Tory, which have so long infested our politics, says, in his pamphlet of 'Faults on both Sides,' " That the former were most suc- " cessful in making proselytes of men of
" thought

" thought and understanding; whilst the latter
" enlisted under their banners those who were
" dissipated and profligate, and looked no far-
" ther than the surface of things."

SIR GODFREY KNELLER.

By the kindness of the Rev. Mr. Green, rector of St. Lawrence's in Reading, the following curious particulars of Sir Godfrey are presented to the public:

" In August 1772, Dr. Pearce, Bishop
" of Rochester, related to my father the fol-
" lowing anecdotes of Sir Godfrey Kneller,
" which were told to the bishop by himself:

" When he (Sir G.) was a young man at
" Venice, he stopped one day to hear a
" mountebank harangue a croud, who im-
" mediately broke off in the midst of his dis-
" course, and looked at him so stedfastly and
" earnestly, that the eyes of the spectators
" were all turned upon him, and then cried
" out, Behold a happy countenance! This
" young man will go to a happy island,
" where he will attain great credit and riches,
" and live to a considerable age; and, to
" prove

"prove all this, if he stays in this city a
"month longer, he will save the life of a
"person who will be condemned innocently.
"He did stay the month; and, during that
"time, painted the wife of one of the pro-
"curators of St. Mark, which picture gave
"so much satisfaction to his employer, that,
"at Sir Godfrey's request, he respited the
"execution of a condemned criminal for a
"month, and during that time the real mur-
"derer was discovered, and the innocent
"person saved. Sir Godfrey came to Eng-
"land, where the remainder of the prophecy
"was fulfilled.

"Sir Godfrey told the Bishop, that he had
"naturally a military genius; and when-
"ever he had the head-ache, if he took a
"pinch of gunpowder, it cured him.

"He gave the following as his articles of
"religion:

"1st. That God Almighty was the most
"ingenious of all beings.

"2dly. That therefore he loved all inge-
"nious persons.

"3dly.

" 3dly. That painting was the most inge-
" nious of all arts, as it preserved for cen-
" turies the remembrance of deceased persons.

" 4thly. That he himself was the most in-
" genious of all painters.

" The bishop one day visiting Sir Godfrey
" at his country-seat at Whitton near Houn-
" flow, he carried him into his summer-
" house, where was a whole length picture of
" Lady Kneller, which was much damaged
" and scratched at the bottom; upon his
" Lordship's expressing a curiosity to know
" how it became so injured, Sir Godfrey said,
" it was owing to a favourite dog of Lady
" Kneller's, who, having been accustomed to
" lie in her lap, scratched the picture in that
" manner in order to be taken up: this made
" the bishop mention that Xeuxis, having
" painted a bunch of grapes upon a boy's
" head so naturally that a bird pecked at them,
" Sir Godfrey answered, That if the boy had
" been painted as well as the grapes, the bird
" would not have ventured to peck at them."

LORD

LORD CHIEF JUSTICE HOLT.

In the reign of Queen Anne, 1704, several freemen of the borough of Aylesbury had been refused the liberty of voting at an election for a member of parliament, though they proved their qualifications as such. The law in this case imposes a fine on the returning officer of 100 l. for every such offence. On this principle they applied to Lord Chief Justice Holt, who ordered the officer to be arrested. The House of Commons, alarmed at this step, made an order of their house to make it penal for either judge, council, or attorney, to assist at the trial: however, the Lord Chief Justice, and several lawyers, were hardy enough to oppose this order, and brought it on in the court of King's Bench. The House, highly irritated at this contempt of their order, sent a serjeant at arms for the judge to appear before them; but that resolute defender of the laws bade him, with a voice of authority, be gone; on which they sent a second message by their speaker, attended by as many members as espoused the measure. After the Speaker had delivered his message, his Lordship replied to him in the following remarkable words: " Go back to
" your

"your chair, Mr. Speaker, within these five
"minutes, or, you may depend on it, I'll
"send you to Newgate. You speak of your
"authority; but I'll tell you I sit here as an
"interpreter of the laws and a distributor of
"justice *, and were the whole House of
"Commons in your belly, I would not stir
"one foot." The Speaker was prudent
enough to retire, and the House were equally
prudent in letting the affair drop.

LORD PETERBOROUGH.

By the kindness of the amiable and elegant Mrs. Lock, of Norbury Park, the following letter of Lord Peterborough to that intelligent foreign minister Sir Luke Schaub is permitted to decorate this COLLECTION:

* It seems strange that the right of voting at elections, like all other rights, should not be decided in our courts of law. The decision would be speedier, attended with less trouble and waste of time, the process would be more dignified and serious, and the judgment pronounced with greater solemnity by persons used to evidence and to legal decisions on all points †.

† An acute criminal said, " If the trial of Mr.
" Hastings," which lasted nearly as long as the siege of
Troy, " had taken place in his court, it would have been
over in twelve days."

" Sir,

"Sir, I wish you a good journey, and all possible succeſſe. I flatter myſelf with happy events, if our united endeavours can prevail with the Spaniards to be wiſe.

"If you give my letter yourſelf to the lady to whom it is addreſſed, you will not be diſpleaſed. Her houſe is agreeable, her converſation eaſy; the moments of leiſure may be ſpent there with ſatisfaction. You may meet with Chriſtians who are ſocial and amuſing; but pray ſpare the Mahometane: for ſhe is, or I wiſh ſhe were, appropriated to the old embaſſador, and your humble ſervant,

"PETERBOROUGH*."

* This nobleman is thus deſcribed in a letter from Cardinal du Bois to Sir Luke Schaub:

"My Lord Peterborough, quoique bien peint dans votre lettre fera plus de mal en France que ne feroit ſon portrait, ſes declamaions impoſent aux ignorans & aux gens mal intentionés & il fait des portraits† de ſa patrie qui font croire a ceux qui l'ecoutent qu'elle n'a pas aucune reſource. On ſe conjecteroit s'il n' n'etoit qu' importun; mais je vous aſſure qu'il fait plus de mal à l' Angleterre pendant ſon ſéjour en France qu'il ne lui en pourvoit en faire a Londres & dans la Chambre des Seigneurs.

"Janvier 27, 1721."

† Lord Peterborough was then in oppoſition to miniſtry.

Dr.

Dr. Freind, in his remarks on the conduct of this intrepid nobleman, says, " that he never sent out a hundred men on any expedition without accompanying them himself."

The great Lord Granville said, " That one day, after Lord Peterborough had received the thanks of the House of Lords, he got into his coach, and stopped at a poulterer's to buy him a fowl, to take home with him to have dressed for his dinner." Lord Granville's coach followed his, and the owner of it, with his usual good-nature, asked Lord Peterborough to his house to dine with him, and drink a bottle of claret with him.

Lord Peterborough had long been married to that excellent and accomplished woman, Anastasia Robinson, before he thought fit to own her for his wife. One evening, however, in the Rooms at Bath, completely to divulge the secret, he called out at the door where the servants were waiting, " Lady Peterborough's chair!" This noble method of treating her she amply compensated to him at his death, by preventing the publication of his manuscript ' Memoirs,' in which he had confessed he had been guilty of three capital crimes before he was one-and-twenty.

LORD GALWAY

gave this excellent advice to Lord Chesterfield: "If you intend to be a man of business, you "must be an early riser*. In the distin- "guished parts your rank and fortune will "lead you to fill, you will be liable to have "visitors every hour of the day; and, unless "you rise constantly at an early hour, you "will never have any time for yourself."

Bishop Porteous says, in his excellent Life of Archbishop Secker; "He rose at six the "whole year round, and had often spent a "busy day before others began to enjoy it."

LORD

---

* A very eminent advocate and great scholar of our times rises very early by this stratagem: He pays his hair-dresser very handsomely to come to dress him nearly at day-break every morning in winter and summer. When the frizeur knocks at the door, no one but the master himself is permitted to let him in. His good-nature, no less than his desire to improve himself, arouses him from his bed, and he descends and opens the door for him. Being once up, and the bands of sleep once burst asunder, he proceeds to his business, and to his studies, with that ardour and felicity of effect, that have ever distinguished his literary character on the great variety of subjects which he has treated.

"If any one," says the Rev. Mr. John Wesley, the late celebrated preacher, "wishes to know what quantity of "sleep

LORD BOLINGBROKE.

When the French prophets came over to England in the time of Queen Ann, and declared that they would raife to life a dead man at the Weft end of St. Paul's Church, the miniftry were alarmed, and were inclined to pre-

" fleep his own fituation requires, he may eafily make the
" experiment which I made fixty years ago. I then waked
" every night about twelve or one o'clock, and lay awake
" for fome time. I readily concluded that this arofe from
" my lying in bed longer than nature required. To be
" fatisfied, I procured an alarum which wakened me the
" next morning at feven, near an hour earlier than I rofe
" the morning before, yet I lay awake again at night; the
" fecond morning I rofe at fix, but notwithftanding this I
" lay awake the fecond night. The third morning I rofe
" at five, but neverthelefs I lay awake the third night. The
" fourth morning I rofe at four (as by the grace of God I
" have done ever fince), and I lay awake no more; and I now
" do not lie awake in the night, taking the year round, a
" quarter of an hour together in a month. By the fame expe-
" riment (rifing earlier and earlier every morning) a man may
" come to know how much fleep he really wants." The
quantity of fleep in general required Mr. Wefley puts at
fix hours, and adds, " that the difference between rifing at
" five and at feven o'clock in the morning for the fpace of
" forty years, fuppofing a man to go to bed every night at
" the fame hour, is equivalent to the addition of ten years
" to a man's life."—*Wefley's Sermon on the Duty and Advantage of early Rifing.*

vent their assembling together in so public a place. Bolingbroke very wisely differed from them, and insisted on their being permitted to play their tricks in the place they intended, merely on account of its publicity. " You " will then," said he, " prevent their assem-
". bling in private ; the consequence of which
" would have been that they would have assured
" the world that they had raised the person
" from the dead as they pretended; and no one
" except those of their own persuasion would
" have been present to have seen whether they
" had done so or not *."

Lord Bolingbroke says in one of his letters to Lord Strafford, " It is a melancholy consi-
" deration, that the laws of our country are too
" weak to punish effectually those factious scrib-
" blers that blacken the brightest characters,
" and give even scurrilous language to those
" who are in the highest degrees of honour.
" This is, amongst others, my dear lord, a

---

* " But these prophets," says the acute and learned Dr. Jortin, " were at last put not out of countenance (for " such persons never blush) but to flight, when they had " failed of their promise to raise a dead man, and had fallen " out among themselves. There will in all probability," adds the Doctor, " be a succession of such persons in every " age in one part or other of the Christian world, not " exactly alike nor yet very different."

" symptom

" symptom of the decayed condition of our
" government, and serves to shew how fatally
" we mistake *licentiousness* for liberty."

DEAN SWIFT.

By the kindness of that excellent instructor of youth, the Rev. Dr. Valpy, of Reading, the following Letter of Dean Swift is permitted to decorate this Collection. It exhibits that singular character in a more amiable point of view than that in which he is generally seen.

" Sir,   London, *April* 13, 1713.

" I am ashamed to tell you how ill a phi-
" losopher I am, and that a very ill situation
" of my affairs for three weeks past made me
" utterly incapable of answering your ob-
" liging letter, or thanking you for your most
" agreeable copy of verses. The prints will
" tell you that I am condemned again to live
" in Ireland; and all that the court and mi-
" nistry did for me was to let me choose my
" situation in the country where I am ba-
" nished. I could not forbear shewing both
" your letter and verses to our great men, as
"   " well

" well as to the men of wit of my acquaint-
" ance, and they were highly approved by
" all. I am altogether a stranger to your
" friend Oppian; and am a little angry when
" those who have a genius lay it out in tranf-
" lations. I queſtion whether ' *Res anguſta*
" *domi*' be not one of your motives. Perhaps
" you want fuch a bridle as a tranſlation, for
" your genius is too fruitful, as appears by
" the frequency of your ſimiles; and this
" employment may teach you to write ' like a
" modeſt man,' as Shakeſpear expreſſeth it.

" I have been minding my Lord Boling-
" broke, Mr. Harcourt, and Sir William
" Windham, to ſollicite my Lord Chancellor
" to give you a living, as a buſineſs which
" belongs to our ſociety, who aſſume the title
" of rewarders of merit. They are all very
" well diſpoſed, and I ſhall not fail to nego-
" ciate for you while I ſtay in England, which
" will not be above ſix weeks; but I hope to
" return in October; and if you are not then
" provided for, I will move heaven and earth
" that ſomething may be done for you. Our
" ſociety hath not met of late, elſe I would
" have moved to have two of us ſent in form
" to requeſt a living for you from my Lord
" Chancellor; and if you have any way to

" employ

" employ my services, I desire you will let me know it, and believe me to be very sincerely,

"Sir,

"Your most faithful humble servant,

"J. Swift,

"To the Reverend Mr. William Diaper,
"Dean, near Basingstoke, Hampshire."

GEORGE II.
KING OF ENGLAND.

During the rebellion of 1745, this intrepid and excellent prince came one day to council later than usual; and having asked the subject of their deliberations, was told that they had been taking measures to ensure the safety of his Majesty's person. "Take care of yourselves, Gentlemen," said he; "for I am resolved to die King of England."

He was much displeased when his civil list happened to be in arrear. This, however, occurred in Mr. Pelham's administration, and he sent for that minister in a great passion, and asked him how this happened. He was told that

that the money appropriated to that service was wanted for more important purposes at that time. " Mr. Pelham," said he, " I will " not be the only gentleman in England " whose servants are not paid; and if you " will not get me the money to pay them, " somebody else shall *."

His Majesty was anxious to pardon Lord Balmerino at the close of the rebellion in 1745, and nobly said, that there had been too much blood spilled already.

Courage and mercy seem hereditary in our present race of sovereigns. In the disgraceful riots of 1780 the property and the buildings of the metropolis were preserved by the spirited behaviour of the present sovereign †, whose

---

* The sovereign's servants are appointed to be paid out of a certain sum of money allowed by parliament to defray the expences of the civil list, which are in fact those of the whole executive power of England; with that the sovereign has nothing to do. The King's privy purse, which is now about sixty thousand pounds a year, is appropriated to his private expences, and may be called the King's pocket money. Out of the privy purse, it is said, near thirty thousand pounds a year are at present destined to charities and benevolences of a private nature.

† See ADDENDA at the end of this Volume.

constant

constant desire to save the lives of his subjects, makes him ever anxious to extend that heavenly boon of his crown, mercy, to as many criminals condemned to death as is consistent with as salutary a virtue, justice; and renders him extremely cautious in investigating the trials of those convicts in which there happen to be any doubts or difficulty: he humanely thinking with the poet,

—————— *audi;*
Nulla unquam de vitâ hominis cunctatio longa est.
JUVENAL.

Had every sovereign in Europe watched over the lives and properties of his people with the same paternal and anxious care, what pretences could those whom they governed have had to fear for their liberties, or to have asserted them in a manner so strenuous and violent as most certainly to risk, and perhaps lose entirely, the very blessings they were so much in earnest to preserve.

SIR ROBERT WALPOLE,

LORD ORFORD.

This great Minister kept up for many years a secret correspondence with Cardinal Fleury; and when Lord Waldegrave waited on the Cardinal to express Sir Robert's wish that it might be continued, and to assure his Eminence of his respect for his character, the Cardinal expatiated on Sir Robert's distinguished abilities, on his integrity, and on his spirit; " characteristicks," as Mr. Coxe says, " highly necessary in the composition of a " great minister *." After his retirement from public business, Sir Robert made so impressive and so loyal a speech in the House of Peers in favour of supporting the house of Hanover, and of immediately attending to the communication of George the Second respecting the intelligence he had of the Pretender's design to invade England, that Frederick, Prince of Wales, rose from his seat and took Sir Robert by the hand, adding many handsome speeches on his loyal effusions.

* See Coxe's ' Memoirs of Sir Robert Walpole.'

Sir

Sir Robert's general principle as a minister was, " *Quieta non movere* * ; to let well alone." He possessed no vain desire to distinguish himself by peculiarity of opinion or hardiness of enterprize, and he detested war. This made the late acute Dr. Johnson (who was no friend to his political opinions) say of him, " He " was the best minister this country ever had ; " as, if *we* would have let him" (he speaks of his own violent faction) " he would have " kept the country in perpetual peace." His celebrated excise scheme his very enemies, after his death, were the first to applaud ; and that acute and honest politician, Dr. Tucker, calls it " a scheme by which the " whole island would have been one free port, " and a magazine and common storehouse " for all nations."

Sir Robert was so little agitated by the attacks that were made upon him, that, like the great Chancellor Oxenstiern, he never lost a night's rest on account of public business. His son, the late ingenious Earl of Orford, has often said, that his father, after the latest and

---

* When Sir William Keith proposed to Sir Robert to tax America he replied, " I have Old England already set " against me ; and do you think I will have New England " likewife ?"

the

the moſt worrying night he ever had in the Houſe of Commons, had fallen into a ſound ſleep before his ſervant had left the room.

Lord Orford made an exquiſite collection of paintings, which were permitted to be ſent out of this country, almoſt to the Pole, for thirty-five thouſand pounds. They contained one of the fineſt pictures that Guido ever painted, the Diſpute of the Doctors of the Church reſpecting the Immaculate Conception of the Virgin*. It was valued at three thouſand five hundred pounds; and in the opinion of an excellent judge, the late Sir Joſhua Reynolds, was not appreciated too highly for its merit. Lord Orford's ſon, with honeſt and yet modeſt indignation, thus ſpeaks of the ſale of his father's pictures: " Having lived un-
" happily to ſee the *nobleſt ſchool* of painting
" that this kingdom ever beheld tranſported
" almoſt out of the ſight of Europe, it would
" be a ſtrange faſcination, nay a total inſen-
" ſibility to the pride of family, and the moral
" reflections that wounded pride commonly
" feels, to expect that a paper fabric, and an

---

* The Pope's antiquarian at firſt refuſed to let it go out of Rome; but when his Holineſs knew that the picture was deſtined for the Prime Miniſter of England, he took off the inhibition.

" aſſemblage

" assemblage of curious trifles made by an
" insignificant person, should last longer, or
" be treated with more veneration and respect
" than the trophies of a palace, deposited in
" it by one of the wisest and best ministers
" that this country has enjoyed."—*Preface to
the Account of Lord Orford's Collection at Straw-
berry Hill.*

Letter of Sir Robert Walpole *to* Sir Luke Schaub: *Printed from the* Original *in the Possession of* Mrs. Lock.

" Sir,   *June* 6, 1723.
" My Lord Carteret has notified to you in
" form the honour the King has done me in
" appointing me one of his principal secre-
" taries of state, and giving you the proper
" orders for transmitting to me duplicates of
" all the dispatches to Hanover, and such
" other advices and accounts as you shall
" learn from time to time, and may be of use
" and service to his Majesty to be communi-
" cated to me.

" I take this first opportunity of beginning
" a correspondence with you, which I hope
" will not be confined to the common forms
" of business, but improved and carried on to
" the utmost confidence. Your residence is
                                         " at

"at the chief place of action in all Europe;
"and your zeal and diligence in his Majesty's
"service so well known and approved, that I
"am confident nothing will slip your notice
"wherein his Majesty's interest is in any
"degree concerned or may be affected; and
"as I am honoured here with the King's
"commands in the manner you are sensible
"of, I am very solicitous that I may be able
"to discharge the trust his Majesty has re-
"posed in me to his satisfaction; and in this
"I am persuaded I shall have all the assistance
"that is in your power to give me, which
"you may be assured I will by all possible
"means endeavour to deserve.

"I hope, Sir, the peace and quiet of the
"kingdom will not be disturbed during his
"Majesty's absence with any new alarms at
"home or from abroad; but if you can discover
"any the least tendency or motion of that
"kind, I desire you will give me the earliest
"notice that is possible of it.

"I send you inclosed a copy of the letter
"that is come to my hands since his Majesty's
"departure; you will be pleased to inform
"yourself of the matters contained in it; and
"whether

" whether there are any grounds of appre-
" henfion that deferve regard.

" Lord Townfhend has recommended to
" my care an affair which you and Mr. Craw-
" ford are acquainted with, concerning fome
" actions of Mr. Law, that are made a fecu-
" rity to Lords Londonderry and Middleton.
" I fhall be able in a few days to give a further
" account of it, and muft defire you in Lord
" Townfhend's and my name to ufe your beft
" offices to ferve the gentleman concerned.

" I believe by this time my fon will be
" come out of Italy to Paris; I give you the
" trouble of this inclofed for him, or, if he is
" not yet arrived, to keep it till you hear he is
" at Paris.

" I muft beg you will make my beft com-
" pliments to the Cardinal *; and if I thought
" it poffible that he fhould want any affurance
" of my unalterable refolutions to preferve and
" cultivate to the utmoft of my power the
" good underftanding and friendfhip that are
" between the two crowns, I fhould defire

* Fleury.

" you

PURCELL

"you in the strongest manner to give him in
"my name all possible assurance of my steady
"adherence to the measures his Majesty is
"engaged in; and I must desire in particular,
"that you will prevail with his Eminence
"to believe that nobody has a greater honour
"and regard for him than I shall upon all
"occasions endeavour to demonstrate; and
"you, Sir, I hope will depend upon the sin-
"cere friendship and best services that are in
"the power of, Sir,

"Your most faithful humble servant,

"R. WALPOLE.

"*Sir Luke Schaub.*"

~~~~~

PURCELL.

FOR the following anecdotes and characters of this great musician and of Handel, the Compiler is indebted to the elegant pen of his friend DR. BURNEY.

" Every English musician that is well ac-
" quainted with the works of Purcell is
" proud of being his countryman. He was,
" indeed, the creator of our dramatic music;
"for

" for anthems and services he had good mo-
" dels in the venerable Tallis, Bird, Mosley,
" Gibbons, and Child; but for secular com-
" positions he had the whole to invent. An
" Italian opera had never been attempted here
" in his time; Lulli's compositions were in
" great favour in many parts of Europe besides
" France, and Purcell seems to have imitated
" his recitative; but for his airs he had no-
" thing to imitate. He found our secular
" music, both vocal and instrumental, in a
" truly barbarous state. Indeed there was
" little melody at that time, except old na-
" tional tunes, in Europe. Purcell had suf-
" ficient good taste to see the merit of Stra-
" della's and Carissimi's elegant simplicity, of
" which he would probably have availed him-
" self more if he had not been obliged to
" deform his melodies by writing down graces
" for ignorant fingers (and *what are called*
" *graces in music, like capricious fashions, be-*
" *come obsolete and ridiculous very soon.*) Co-
" relli's elegant simplicity procured a longe-
" vity to his productions of which none of
" his countrymen were possessed. There is
" no coeval Italian instrumental music that
" is now bearable.

" The

"The church music of Purcell is still the most interesting which our cathedrals can boast. It is replete with learning, without labour or pedantry. His dramatic music, for which Dryden often furnished the poetry, is admirable to all those who can for a moment mount up to the period of his existence. His correct accentuation of words, and expression of the sentiments they contain, are so congenial to the ears and feelings of unprejudiced Englishmen, that his melodies go by a more straight road to the heart than much more modern and polished music. Many passages that now seem on paper to be old fashioned and uncouth, have this effect when sung.

"His catches have continued for more than a hundred years to be the models of ingenuity and humour in that species of convivial composition; and it will be long ere they are supplanted by superior productions of the same kind.

"As an amiable and pleasing man he has been as much celebrated as for his professional abilities *. The writer of this article

"is

---

* Dr. B. is in possession of an original drawing of Purcell by Sir Godfrey Kneller, in which there is a glow of beauty,

"is old enough to remember the affectionate
"rapture with which he was mentioned by
"those who knew him personally. Handel
"lived in a more polished age, and had to dis-
"play the talents of performers of a much
"higher class than those for whom Purcell
"composed; but it may, perhaps, admit of a
"dispute which was gifted with the largest
"portion of innate genius; had Handel been
"Purcell, and Purcell Handel, with equal lon-
"gevity, it may be doubted whether the public
"would have received more pleasure from
"either of their productions. Handel moved
"in a wider sphere, and travelled the grand
"high road to fame. Purcell moved on a
"more contracted scale, and arrived at her
"temple by a more private road; but he can-
"not be said to have lost his way: He *did*
"arrive there, and had an honourable niche
"assigned him, though not in so conspicuous
"a place as Handel justly obtained."

beauty, expression, and genius above humanity; it might with propriety pass for the head of Apollo. It is engraven for this COMPILATION.

HANDEL.

HANDEL.

"It is frequently found in the biography
"of great men, that they have purfued by
"ftealth a courfe of ftudy totally different
"from that which was deftined them by their
"friends.

"Among great aftronomers Copernicus was
"intended for a phyfician; Tycho Brahe for
"jurifprudence; Pafcal, when a child, could
"not be prevented from becoming a geome-
"trician, in fpite of his father's wifhes to keep
"him back; Euler, intended for the church,
"relinquifhed the ftudy of theology for that
"of mathematics, contrary to the defire of his
"family; nor could Handel, intended for the
"profeffion of the civil law, be deterred by his
"father from the ftudy of mufic furrepti-
"tioufly, even before he was allowed a mafter,
"or arrived at feven years of age. He was
"certainly a great performer on the organ
"and a good contrapuntift before he went to
"Italy at four-and-twenty; but it was there,
"by the compofitions of Cariffimi, the elder
"Scarlatti, and Corelli, that he refined his
"tafte in melody; and by the ftudy and
"practice of the Italian language, and the
"performance

"performance of great theatrical singers, that
"he qualified himself for composing Italian
"operas, and for being selected, in preference
"to all the masters in Europe, to compose
"and superintend, under the auspices of
"the *Royal Academy*, the Italian opera in
"London *.

"It seems manifest that Handel continued
"to change and improve his vocal melody
"from the taste and talents of the great
"singers who successively arrived in England
"during the existence of the Royal Aca-
"demy, and his own opera regency. Thus
"we see the songs composed for *Nicolini,
"Senesino, Caristini, Boschi*, the *Cuzzoni, Fauf-
"tina*, and *Strada*, all in different styles, to
"suit their peculiar powers and compass of
"voice, and here we have his most flowery
"melodies and proofs of his inventive powers.
"But in composing *Te Deums, Anthems,* and
"*Oratorios*, his immortal chorusses, the off-
"spring of profound knowledge and study.

* In his way to England, after his journey to Italy, Handel, at Hanover, sat for his picture to the celebrated German painter *Wolfgang*. Dr. Burney is in possession of this valuable portrait; it is a half length, and there are many persons still living who remember the great musician very like this picture.

"chiefly

" chiefly occupied his attention; the folo airs
" being often compoſed for ordinary fingers,
" he was obliged to degrade his fancy to the
" level of the performers for whom he had to
" write, and to confider, not what he could
" invent, but what they could execute. He
" had, indeed, Franceſſina ſome time; and
" Fraſi and Galli, never opera performers of
" the firſt claſs, were the beſt fingers for whom
" he had to compoſe; the reſt were little
" better than ballad fingers, except Mrs. Cib-
" ber, who without knowledge of muſic, by
" thoroughly feeling and comprehending the
" words, and by a natural pathetic expreſſion
" and touching tone of voice, was enabled
" to ſing the two divine airs of ' He was
" deſpiſed,' in the *Meſſiah*; and ' Return, O
" God of Hoſts,' in *Sampſon*, with more ef-
" fect than any of the greateſt opera fingers,
" with all their ſkill and refinements, could
" produce. Handel in his choruſſes, befides
" the ſuperior merit of fugue and learned
" counterpoint, is a great painter; not merely
" by delineating obvious and common paſ-
" ſions and ideas, but by awakening in the
" mind ſenſations which ſeemed out of the
" reach of muſical expreſſion; particularly in
" *Iſrael in Egypt*, where the choruſſes, next to
" thoſe in the *Meſſiah*, are the moſt original,

" impreſſive,

"impressive, and surprising. Other indivi-
"dual chorusses might be pointed out in all
"his oratorios, such as ' O God, who in thy
"heavenly hand,' in *Solomon*; others in
"*Sampson, Judas Maccabæus, Deborah*, &c.
"are of unrivalled and of infinite merit; but
"as a whole, in no one oratorio are the cho-
"russes so constantly sublime and astonishing
"as in the *Messiah* and *Israel in Egypt*.

"His compositions for the organ, particu-
"larly the six fugues in the first book of his
"*Pieces de Clavecin* are, for pleasing subjects,
"and masterly treatment, perhaps, the most
"perfect productions of that elaborate kind,
"and for that divine instrument, that have
"ever been published.

"His performance on the organ can no
"otherwise be described than by saying that
"it was the most clear, pleasing, and masterly,
"that can be imagined. Full and rich har-
"mony, but never tinctured by crude, pe-
"dantic, and affected modulation; availing
"himself of the genius and powers of the in-
"strument, the chain of kindred sounds was
"never broken; his fingers seemed to grow
"to the keys, and all the harmonic relations
"to be combined and preserved from the
"beginning of a movement to the end.

"Of

"Of his probity, bluntness, wit, humour, and original pleasantry, nothing is left to be said. His piety can never be doubted by those who hear his divine strains, which make others feel too much, not to assure us that he felt the sacred subject he had to treat himself. In short, he was in all things an extraordinary man; not only for his professional abilities, but for his spirit, fortitude, manners, grotesque images, and original ideas."

Though Dr. Burney has so amply reviewed the works of Handel in his 'History of Music,' and enthusiastically pointed out the extraordinary merit of those pieces that were selected for his Commemoration, in the excellent account he has given of that celebration, at the request of the Sovereign *, the COMPILER could not help requesting him to go over the ground again, and to furnish him with some account of that great musician for the present COLLECTION. Such an account, indeed, might have been easily extracted from the works just mentioned; but he wished that the merits of Handel might be impressed on the minds of his rea-

* To this book he has prefixed a Sketch of the Life of Handel.

ders by one infinitely more capable of doing them justice than himself, and whose eminent knowledge of the subject leaves him without appeal.

DR. MEAD.

This great physician was a man of various and extensive learning, and supported with great success the character for general knowledge and polite letters for which his predecessors in his own useful and honourable art in England have been ever distinguished.

He wrote with great science, and with extreme elegance, on the medical subjects which he treated. His 'Essay on the Influence of the Sun and Moon upon Human Bodies' was strenuously opposed at first. Since his death the observations contained in it have been nearly verified; and in this instance, as in many others, the truth has been found to lie between the two extremes; and time, the patient and the unprejudiced judge of all matters in dispute, has done justice to Dr. Mead's opinions.

This great investigator of nature died with the same tranquillity with which he lived. Not many hours before he breathed his last,

he

he was employed in reading one of Cicero's philosophical pieces.

" During almost half a century," says his biographer, " he was at the head of his business, which brought him in one year upwards of seven thousand pounds. His generous and benevolent temper was constantly exercised in acts of charity. Clergymen, and in general all men of learning, were welcome to his advice; and his doors were open every morning to the most indigent, whom he frequently assisted with his purse."

" Ingenious men," adds he, " were sure of finding at Dr. Mead's the best helps in almost all their undertakings. Nothing pleased him more than to be the voice of any thing that could call every hidden talent into light, to give encouragement to the greatest projects, and to see them executed under his own eyes. Scarce any thing curious hath appeared in England since the beginning of this century but under his patronage. He continually kept in his pay a great number of scholars, and of artists of all kinds, who were continually at work for him, or rather for the public.
" As

" As he was a perfect judge of whatever was
" excellent, and as he admitted nothing elfe
" into his collection,. fo he always purchafed
" it at its value."

" Nothing did more honour to this patron of
" learning than the free and conftant accefs of
" men of different qualifications to his table,
" who were each employed the reft of the day
" at his particular work or ftudy. No foreigner
" of any learning, tafte, or even curiofity, ever
" came to London without being introduced to
" Dr. Mead: it would have been difgraceful to
" return home without having feen him. On
" thefe occafions his table was always open, and
" he united the magnificence of a prince with
" the refinement of a philofopher. Every
" one found himfelf furrounded with objects
" capable of inftructing or of amufing him.
" Our Mecænas was frequently the only
" man in company who was acquainted with
" all their different languages, and was able to
" perform the office of interpreter to them all.
" He conftantly queftioned them, in a moft
" obliging manner, about their different occu-
" pations, taking great pleafure in commending
" their feveral performances and difcoveries,
" and by this means infpired them with emu-
" lation and a natural efteem for each other.
" There

" There no man's talents were misplaced, none was honoured with an undue preference. The scholar took his place near the naturalist, and the mathematician near the antiquarian or the painter. Every one found himself surrounded with objects capable of instructing him or exciting his emulation.

" His library was open to every one who wished to consult it, and he permitted his books to be taken out of it, for the use of his friends and of the learned *."

" Dr. Mead," said the present illustrious Father of Physic in this country, " by his extensive and varied learning, his extreme generosity, and the elegance of his manners, dignified the profession which he exercised;"† a very high compliment indeed to Mead,

---

* Whoever has the honour to know Sir Joseph Banks will perceive in many parts of Dr. Mead's character a similarity between him and the present liberal and active President of the Royal Society.

† " I intend," says Bishop Warburton, in one of his MS. letters, " to send one of my pamphlets to Dr. Mead, " as a man to whom all persons who pretend to letters " ought to pay their tribute, on account of his great knowledge in them, and extensive patronage of them."

which

which posterity will not fail amply to repay to Dr. Heberden *.

It is said that Mead, when very young, consulted Dr. Radcliffe on the means of rising in his profession. " There are two ways of " doing so," replied that sagacious and extensive practitioner, " by bullying or cajoling " mankind. I have bullied them, and have " done very well, as you see; you, perhaps, " will cajole them, and that may do full as " well."

LORD CHANCELLOR HARDWICKE.

For the following account of this great magistrate the COMPILER is obliged to a learned Advocate:

" The Earl of Hardwicke was certainly one " of the greatest ornaments of the English na-

* A friend of Dr. Heberden, on hearing of the accident of his fall, which in some degree has embittered the latter part of his honourable, useful, and virtuous life, exclaimed from Virgil,

—————— *nec te tua plurima, Pantheu,*
Labentem pietas, nec Apollinis infula texit!

" tion,

" tion. He was born in very humble life, com-
" mencing his legal career in the lowest walk of
" the profession; but, uniting uncommon abi-
" lities with uncommon industry, advanced him-
" self to the highest office of the English judi-
" cature, and to the dignity of a peer of Great
" Britain. He acquired an immense fortune,
" and obtained for his sons some of the first
" offices in church and state. It is observable,
" that his Lordship, and his great contempo-
" rary the Earl of Mansfield, differed extremely
" in their mode of fructifying their money; the
" former investing it immediately in the pur-
" chase of land, the latter placing it out upon
" mortgage. In the event, the mode adopted
" by Lord Hardwicke proved most productive,
" the increase of the value of land, and the
" advance of rents, greatly counterbalancing
" the advantage of 5 per cent. interest. In the
" years 1740, 1748, and 1752, his Lordship
" was appointed one of the Lords Justices for
" the administration of the government during
" King George the Second's absence on his
" journies in those years to his German domi-
" nions. In 1749, he was unanimously chosen
" high steward of the university of Cambridge.
" In 1736-7, he was appointed lord high chan-
" cellor of England, and held that office till
" 1756, when he resigned the seals, to the great

" concern

"concern of the bar, and, as it was said at the
"time, to the great mortification of the king.
"The period during which he presided in
"chancery is an æra in the judicature of that
"court. The bar was never more respectable;
"but the superior powers of his Lordship were
"universally felt and acknowledged; and, ex-
"cept some petulant expressions which fell from
"Lord Chief Justice Willes, when he was called
"to his assistance in the case of Omychund
"against Barker, his Lordship was treated in
"his court with a degree of respect that bor-
"dered nearly on veneration. He was most
"patient in hearing a cause, almost always
"pronounced immediate judgment upon it,
"and very seldom postponed his decisions from
"one term to another. In his arguments
"from the bench his language was easy and
"dignified; he displayed a profusion of legal
"learning; his mode of applying it was lu-
"minous, and his conclusions carried con-
"viction. Three appeals only were made
"from his decrees, and in these his decisions
"were confirmed. A determination of Lord
"Hardwicke is, to this day, the very highest
"authority that can be urged in any court of
"equity. He had three sons. Philip, his
"eldest son, and his successor in his title, was
"a man of learning and taste, and is supposed
"to have contributed greatly to the publica-
"tion

" tion called ' The Athenian Letters.' The
" celebrated Mr. Charles Yorke was his Lord-
" ship's second son.

" The following is a copy of the introduc-
" tory part of the will of Mr. Charles Yorke:

" Being lately called upon, by the death
" of my most affectionate and entirely be-
" loved wife, to reflect on the uncertainty of
" all enjoyments in this world, I think it an
" act of duty and prudence to make some
" disposition of my real and personal estate by
" will. But, having mentioned the affecting
" occasion which has turned my thoughts
" to this subject, I ought, in the first place,
" to return my grateful acknowledgments to
" Almighty God (the author of every good
" and perfect gift) for many great mercies
" and unmerited advantages, particularly for
" that greatest of all blessings conferred upon
" me in my marriage with my most amiable
" wife Catherine, whose artless manner,
" sweet temper, tender, generous, and
" disinterested kindness, unaffected piety to
" God, and habitual cheerfulness (the happy
" result of the purest innocence, and the most
" steady principles of religion and virtue),
" made her the delight of all who knew her,
" and

"and an example worthy of imitation. It
"was the goodness of God to indulge me in
"the enjoyment of such a blessing; it was
"his wisdom and righteous will to make that
"enjoyment short, and to take her from me
"in the bloom of her age, and in the midst
"of my best hopes, lest I might feel more
"calmness and prosperity than was good for
"me; being conscious of many frailties, er-
"rors, and transgressions, of which I humbly
"implore his forgiveness, through the merits
"of Jesus Christ my only Saviour; and that
"his providence will graciously deliver me,
"both here and in another state of existence,
"from the evil consequences of them all.
"In the next place, I desire my executors to
"bury me in the same vault at W——, in
"C——shire, with my said dearest * wife and
"my two infant daughters, M. and C. in the
"firm belief and hope of the resurrection of
"the innocent and pure in heart to a blessed
"immortality."

* "The lady so affectionately mentioned by Mr. Yorke,
"was his first wife Catherine, the daughter of the Rev.
"Dr. William Freeman, of Hammells, in Hertfordshire."

LORD

LORD MANSFIELD

was in early life acquainted with the Batchelor Lord Foley, as he was frequently called, who, on his Lordſhip acquainting him that he was afraid he ſhould be obliged to give up the ſtudy of the law, and to go into orders, on account of the ſcantineſs of his income, very nobly requeſted his acceptance of two hundred pounds a year out of the income of five hundred which his father allowed him. Lord Mansfield accepted the offer, and ever afterwards was much attached to the family of Foley.

MR. HOWARD

ſeems, like a genius beneficent to mankind, to have loſt his own life in endeavouring to ſave that of others, and to make the repoſitories of ſuppoſed criminals, what they were, in the humane ſpirit of our laws, intended to have been, repoſitories *in cuſtodiam, non in pœnam.*

He told Mr. Seward, that of the preſence of immediate infection he thought he had a criterion by a pain over his eyes, with a ſenſe of tightneſs. As a preventive againſt its effects, he ſaid he knew of nothing effectual; and that even the Turks themſelves, ſo often viſited by peſtilence,

lence, had no confidence in any particular specific.*

RICHARD FARMER, D.D.

MASTER OF EMMANUEL COLLEGE, AND CANON RESIDENTIARY OF ST. PAUL'S.

For the following character of this ingenious and excellent man the Compiler is indebted to Isaac Reed, Esq. a Collector of great liberality and generosity; a man who, modestly and wisely confining his efforts to one particular branch of literature, has arrived at such a degree of eminence in it, that his lite-

---

* The following mixture, invented by Dr. Carmichael Smyth, has been found nearly a specific against contagion. It has been tried with constant success on board the Russian and British fleets, and in many military and marine hospitals; and by analogy bids fair to stop the contagion of the plague itself:

" Put some heated sand in a small earthen pipkin; in this
" place a tea-cup filled with half an ounce of strong vi-
" triolic acid; when warmed a little, add to it half an
" ounce of purified nitre in powder, stirring the mixture
" with a slip of glass, or the small end of a tobacco-pipe.
" This process should be renewed from time to time; or, if
" you wish to keep up a constant fumigation, it is only
" putting the pipkin over a lamp, or making use of one
" of Mofer's fumigating lamps, made expressly for this
" purpose." See *Dr. Carmichael Smyth's Letter to Lord Spencer, First Lord of the Admiralty.* 8vo.

rary friends are at a loss which to admire most, his power or his inclination to assist them.

"Richard Farmer, D. D. was the architect of
"his own fortune; and without the aid of friends
"or powerful connections elevated himself to an
"honourable and lucrative situation, in the en-
"joyment of which he bounded his ambition at
"a time when he might have obtained higher
"preferment. From his entrance into the Uni-
"versity he seemed to have fixed on Cambridge
"as the place destined for his future residence,
"and uniformly rejected every offer the accept-
"ance of which would occasion his entire re-
"moval from that place. His attention to the
"interests of the town and university never was
"suspended, and by his exertions every improve-
"ment and convenience introduced for the last
"thirty years were either originally proposed or
"ultimately forwarded and carried into execu-
"tion. The plan for paving, watching, and
"lighting the town, after many ineffectual at-
"tempts, was accomplished in his second Vice-
"Chancellorship, greatly to the satisfaction of
"all parties, whose petty objections and jea-
"lousies, and discordant and jarring interests
"he exerted himself with success to obviate, to
"moderate, and to reconcile. As a Magistrate
"he was active and diligent, and on more than
"one

"one occasion of riots displayed great firmness of mind in dangerous conjunctures. As the Master of his College he was easy and accessible, cultivating the friendship of the fellows and inferior members by every mark of kindness and attention; and this conduct was rewarded in the manner he most wished by the harmony which prevailed in the society, and by an entire exemption from those feuds and animosities which too often tore to pieces and disgraced other colleges. In his office of Residentiary of St. Paul's, if he was not the first mover he was certainly the most strenuous advocate for promoting the art of sculpture by the introduction of statuary into the metropolitan cathedral; and many of the regulations on the subject were suggested by him, and adopted in consequence of his recommendation. His literary character rests on one small work, " The Essay on the Learning of Shakspeare," composed in the early period of his life, and which completely settled a much litigated and controverted question, contrary to the opinions of many eminent writers, in a manner that carried conviction to the mind of every one who had either carelessly or carefully reflected on the subject. It may in truth be pointed out as a master-piece, whether considered with a view to the sprightliness

" liness and vivacity with which it is written,
" the clearness of the arrangement, the force
" and variety of the evidence, or the com-
" pression of scattered materials into a narrow
" compass; materials which inferior writers
" would have expanded into a large volume.
" He had no taste for the prevailing pursuit
" in the university, the mathematicks, nor ever
" paid any regard to it after he had obtained
" his first two degrees; but he cultivated the
" belles lettres with great assiduity, though with
" little appearance of regular study. His know-
" ledge of books in all languages, and in every
" science, was very comprehensive. He was
" fond of reading, and continued the habit
" until the last stage of his existence. His
" good humour, liberality, pleasantry, and hos-
" pitality might afford subjects for unmixed
" panegyric to which every one who knew
" him would readily assent. These will live
" in the memory of his surviving friends, who,
" whenever his name occurs, cannot but sigh
" at the reflection that those qualities which
" have so often soothed and gladdened life were
" suffered to exist no longer in the possessor
" than until he had attained the age of sixty-
" two years. He died the 8th September 1797.

" The illiberal practice of the present times
" may expect a drawback of the foibles of a man
" of

"of genius and virtue. That Dr. Farmer had
"some it would be ridiculous to deny and use-
"less to conceal. They were, however, such as
"superseded no duty, encouraged no vice, and
"might pass in review before the most rigid
"moralist without calling for more than a very
"slight censure. In reality they were lost in
"the recollection of his many amiable qualities:
"Some of them, however, are delicately glanced
"at in the following masterly character drawn
"by the Reverend Dr. PARR, and published a
"short time before Dr. Farmer's death:

"Of any undue partiality towards the
"master of Emmanuel college I shall not be
"suspected by those persons who know how
"little his sentiments accord with my own
"upon some ecclesiastical and many political
"matters. From rooted principle and ancient
"habit he is a Tory; I am a Whig; and we
"have both of us too much confidence in
"each other, and too much respect for our-
"selves, to dissemble what we think upon any
"grounds or to any extent. Let me then do
"him the justice which amidst all our dif-
"ferences in opinion I am sure that he will
"ever be ready to do to me. His knowledge
"is various, extensive, and recondite. With
"much seeming negligence, and perhaps in
"later

" later years some real relaxation, he under-
" stands more and remembers more about
" common and uncommon subjects of litera-
" ture, than many of those who would be
" thought to read all the day and meditate
" half the night. In quickness of apprehen-
" sion and acuteness of discrimination I have
" not often seen his equal. Through many a
" convivial hour have I been charmed by his
" vivacity; and upon his genius I have re-
" flected in many a serious moment with
" pleasure, with admiration, but not without
" regret, that he has never concentrated and
" exerted all the great powers of his mind in
" some great work upon some great subject.
" Of his liberality in patronizing learned men
" I could point out numerous instances.
" Without the smallest propensities to ava-
" rice, he possesses a large income; and,
" without the mean submissions of depen-
" dance, he is risen to high station. His am-
" bition, if he has any, is without insolence;
" his munificence is without ostentation; his
" wit is without acrimony; and his learning
" without pedantry."

" Dr. Farmer, when a young man, at the re-
" quest of a friend, wrote the following Direc-
" tions for studying the English history, which,

" with

" with his permission, were printed in his life-
" time in the European Magazine for June
" 1791:

" Dear Sir,

" You will not expect to be sent to the
" authors who are usually called Classical for
" much information on the English History.
" Very little is met with in the Greek, and
" not a great deal in the Latin. Cæsar, Ta-
" citus, and Suetonius, are the only ones
" worth mentioning on this subject.

" Nor will you choose to be referred to the
" Monkish writers. Jeffrey of Monmouth
" and his story of Brute are now generally
" given up. Some of them indeed, as Wil-
" liam of Malmsbury, Matthew Paris, &c.
" have a more authentic character; but I
" suppose any one (except a professed anti-
" quary) will be contented with them at se-
" cond-hand in the modern historians. Carte
" has made the most and best use of them,
" which is the greatest merit of his book.
" Hume often puts their names in his margin;
" but I fear all he knew of them was through
" the *media* of other writers. He has some mis-
" takes, which could not have happened had
" he really consulted the originals.

" The

"The first planting of every nation is ne-
"cessarily obscure, and always lost in a pre-
"tended antiquity. It matters little to us
"whether our island was first peopled by
"Trojans, Phœnicians, Scythians, Celts, or
"Gauls, who have all their respective advo-
"cates; and the famous Daniel de Foe makes
"his 'True-born Englishman' a compound of
"all nations under heaven. If you choose,
"however, to read about this matter, 'She-
"ringham *de Anglorum Origine*,' 8vo. 1670, is
"the best book for the purpose. I may just
"mention, that some writers would cavil at
"the word *island* just above, and insist that
"we were formerly joined to the French
"continent.

"Little real knowledge is to be picked up
"from our history before the Conquest; yet
"it may not be amiss to have a general idea
"of the Druidical government among the
"ancient Britons; of the invasion of the
"Romans under Julius Cæsar, and again in
"the time of Claudius; the struggles for
"liberty under Caractacus, Boadicea, &c.;
"the desertion of the island by the Romans;
"the irruption of the Picts and Scots; the
"calling in of the Saxons as allies; who,
"after a time, turned their arms against the
                                        "natives,

" natives, and conquered them (some few ex-
" cepted, who secured themselves in the
" mountains of Wales, whence their de-
" scendants affect to call themselves Ancient
" Britons); the establishment of the Hep-
" tarchy; &c. the union under King Eg-
" bert; the invasion and various fortunes of
" the Danes; and, lastly, the Normans under
" William the Conqueror.

" The best authors for this period are
" Milton and Sir William Temple; the lat-
" ter more pleasing, but the former more ac-
" curate. Milton's prose works are exceed-
" ingly stiff and pedantic, and Sir William's
" as remarkably easy and genteel; but he
" should have attended more to the *minutiæ*
" of names and dates.

" As to the religion of our ancestors, some-
" thing of the Druids may be learned from
" ' Schedius *de Diis Germanis*,' and an essay in
" ' Toland's Posthumous Works.' Christianity
" seems to have been introduced, perhaps by
" some of the Romans, in the first century.
" Some indeed pretend, that St. Paul himself
" came over.

" The

" The Saxons brought their own gods with
" them, viz. the Sun, Moon, Tuifco, Woden,
" Thor, Friga, and Seater, and, in imitation
" of the Romans, dedicated to them refpec-
" tively the days of the week; and hence the
" names which continue to our times. For
" this fubject I would recommend ' Ver-
" ftegan's Reftitution of decayed Intelli-
" gence.'

" From the Conqueft our annals are more
" clear than thofe of any other nation in the
" world. This happens from the cuftom or
" obligation that every mitred abbey was
" under to employ a regiftrary for all extraordi-
" nary events; and their notes were ufually
" compared together at the end of every
" reign. Hence the great number of Mon-
" kifh hiftorians.

" It luckily happens, that no party-fpirit
" has biaffed the hiftorians in their accounts
" of our old kings; and it therefore does not
" much fignify what author is read. You
" would fmile at my love of black letter, were
" I to refer you to Hollinfhed or Stowe; men,
" I affure you, by no means defpicable, and
" much fuperior to Caxton, Fabian, Graf-
" ton, &c.; nor will you choofe to read
" chro-

"chronicles in rhyme; as Robert of Gloucester and Harding. The moſt elegant old hiſtory we have is that by Samuel Daniel, a poet of no mean rank. Though he wrote more than half a century before Milton, his ſtile appears much more modern. His continuator Truſſel is not ſo well ſpoken of. Daniel is very conciſe in his accounts before the Conqueſt, but much fuller afterwards. He ends with Edward III. and Truſſell with Richard III. This book is reprinted in Biſhop Kennet's 'Collections;' but the old editions are the beſt. The Biſhop employed Oldmixon, a hero of the Dunciad, in the republication; who, we are told, falſified it in many places.

"If we are not content with general accounts of the ſubſequent reigns, it may not be amiſs to look at their particular writers. 'Buck's Hiſtory of Richard III.' is remarkable, from the pains he takes to clear his character againſt the ſcandal (as he calls it) of other hiſtorians. Lord Bacon's florid 'Hiſtory of Henry the Seventh' comes next. You muſt know this king was a favourite with James the Firſt; and, as it was written to recover his favour, the author, you may ſuppoſe, has not been impartial. Lord Herbert's
"'Henry

" ' Henry the Eighth' well deserves reading;
" he was a free thinker and a free writer; his
" information was good, and the era particularly
" interesting. The next work of importance
" (not quite forgetting Dr. afterwards Sir John
" Hayward's ' Edward the Sixth') is ' Cam-
" den's Elizabeth,' a performance worthy of
" its author. The story of Mary Queen of
" Scots may be more particularly learned from
" her countrymen Melvil, Buchanan, &c.

" The Stuarts have brought in a flood of
" histories, many high-flying panegyrics, and
" many scandalous invectives. On James the
" First, Wilson, Saunderson, Weldon, &c.
" and a late writer, one Harris, an Anabap-
" tist parson.

" For Charles the First appears our greatest
" historian Lord Clarendon: on the other
" side Ludlow, who, however, is particularly
" severe on Cromwell. I omit Whitlock,
" Rushworth, Warwick, and a thousand others.

" After the Restoration, Bishop ' Burnet's
" History of his Own Times' will come in,
" and carry us to the end of Queen Anne's
" reign; a curious work, but to be read with
" great

"great caution, as the bishop had strong
"prejudices. Salmon wrote an answer to it.

"Rapin seems the next writer of much
"consequence. Voltaire, certainly a good
"judge of history, calls him our best histo-
"rian; but perhaps he was partial to his coun-
"tryman. It is, however, a work of much
"accuracy, but barren of reflection, and con-
"sequently heavy in the reading. Carte,
"who emphatically stiles himself an English-
"man, wrote purposely against him, on the
"Tory side of the question.

"The later historians, Hume, Smollett,
"&c. you know perhaps as well as I do.
"Hume is certainly an admirable writer; his
"stile bold, and his reflections shrewd and
"uncommon; but his religious and political
"notions have too often warped his judg-
"ment. [Mrs. Macaulay has just now pub-
"lished against his account of the Stuarts;
"but I have not yet had an opportunity of
"reading her book.] Smollett wants the
"dignity of history, and takes every thing
"upon trust; but his books, at least the
"former volumes, are sufficiently pleasing.
"I have purposely omitted a multitude of
                                    "writers;

" writers; as Speed, Baker, Brady, Tyrrel,
" Echard, Guthrie, &c.

" Collections of Letters and State Papers
" are of the utmost importance, if we pretend
" to exactness; such as a collection called
" the 'Cabala,' Burleigh's, Sydney's, Thur-
" loe's, &c.

" The last observation I shall trouble you
" with is, that sometimes a single pamphlet
" will give us better the clue of a transaction
" than a volume in folio. Thus we learn from
" the Duchess of Marlborough's 'Apology,'
" that the peace of Utrecht was made by a
" quarrel among the women of the bed-
" chamber! Hence Memoirs, Secret His-
" tories, Political Papers, &c. are not to be
" despised; always allowing sufficiently for
" the prejudice of the party, and believing
" them no farther than they are supported by
" collateral evidence.

" I remain, &c.
" R. P."

The arts have particular obligations to Dr. Farmer in this country. He opened a new and splendid theatre for their exertions. His good sense pervaded every thing in which he was

was concerned. As Residentiary of St. Paul's he saw but too plainly the desolate state of the fabric, and that, for want of proper decorations, it appeared only to be the most beautiful stone quarry * in Europe. He prevailed upon the Chapter of that cathedral to admit monuments into it, under proper restrictions; and by the wise and liberal regulations that they made, to render it, as Sir Joshua Reynolds exultingly said, " the British Temple of " Fame †." Mr. Howard's monument was the first that was proposed for it; which gave rise to the following judicious observations on sepulchral decorations, which were addressed to the Committee appointed to conduct the business of that monument by the Marquis of Lansdowne:

" In complimenting or commemorating any " great character, expence is a secondary con-

---

* Had the times been more auspicious to matters of taste and of elegance, Mr. Burke, at the suggestion of his friend Sir Joshua Reynolds, intended to have applied to parliament for a certain annual sum to gild the capitals of the columns and other salient parts of the cathedral of St. Paul's.

† The Genius of Taste in vain perambulates this sacred fabric, to find in it the statue of her favourite son Sir Joshua Reynolds, which perhaps, like those of Brutus or of Cassius, in the funeral procession of one of their family, *præfulget, quia non cernitur.*

" sideration.

"sideration. All works of art please or dis-
"please in proportion as taste and judgment
"prevail over it. In architecture, the great-
"ness of the mass sometimes imposes, even
"where the structure is barbarous; but in
"sculpture, the mass becomes an intolerable
"enormity, where it is not highly executed
"and imagined; which, in a groupe of
"figures, implies the arts to have attained the
"utmost degree of perfection. In the case
"of monuments this is the more true, as the
"mere massy monument, composed of com-
"mon-place allegory, may be raised to any
"body, whose will or whose posterity may
"direct the payment for it, without creating
"any interest, and often without being at all
"understood. Besides, the public is in ge-
"neral grown cold to allegory, even in paint-
"ing, where nevertheless it is much more
"supportable than in statuary. The great
"object, where a character admits of it,
"should be to produce those sensations which
"resemblances of exalted characters never
"fail to do, even in persons most experienced
"in the human character; and at the same
" time create an association of ideas, which
' may tell themselves in honour of the persons
"intended to be remembered.

"The

"The proposal for erecting a monument to the late Mr. Howard suggests these reflections. If they have any foundation, it will be difficult to find an occasion so proper, and so free from objection, to inforce and carry them into effect; as, besides continuing his likeness to posterity by a single statue, three public points may be obtained; which, combined all together, must reflect the highest honour on his memory; namely,

"1st, To reserve St. Paul's, the second building in Europe, and the first in Great Britain, from being disfigured or misapplied in the manner of Westminster Abbey.

"2dly, To assist the arts most essentially, by advancing statuary, which may be considered as the first, because it is the most durable, amongst them.

"3dly, To commence a selection of characters, which can alone answer the purpose of rewarding past or exciting future virtues; and the want of which selection makes a public monument scarcely any compliment.

"It would be not only invidious, but unfair, to criticise the several monuments in Westminster Abbey; but let any person of the least feeling, not to mention taste or art, unprejudice his mind, and he must find himself more interested in viewing the single statue erected by Mr. Horace Walpole to his mother Lady Orford, than with any of the piles erected to great men. And if Mrs. Nightingale's monument captivates beyond many others, it is greatly on account of its simplicity, and its being very little more than a single figure. It may as well be supposed that a young person can begin to write whole sentences without making single letters, as that statuaries can make groupes with so little practice as they have in single figures. But if the example is once set, it will most likely become a general fashion to erect statues or busts to every person whose family can afford it, throughout the country. Fifty statues and a hundred busts will be bespoken where one groupe now is; since a statue will probably be to be had for 30 l. and a bust for 5 o l. Besides which, simple tablets may be admitted into country churches, subject to some arrangement, which may answer the purpose of general ornament, and prevent

"churches

" churches from being disfigured, as they now
" universally are. The same reason which
" makes our chimney-pieces better worked,
" and sharper carved, than those which come
" from Rome, namely, the greatness of the
" demand, will gradually improve our artists
" in the more elevated line of their profession.
" Their numbers and their constant employ-
" ment will give a greater chance, if not a
" certainty, of genius discovering itself from
" time to time.

" The selection might be made subject, in
" the first instance,

" 1. To the King's sign manual.

" 2. The vote of either House of Parlia-
" ment.

" 3. The vote of the East India Company.

" 4. The ballot of the Royal Society.

" 5. The sense of any profession, taken
" under such regulations as may be deemed
" most unexceptionable.

" 6. The

" 6. The same as to artists, men of letters, or other descriptions, subject to proper regulations.

" The subscription and the vote must be a sufficient check upon all persons of the latter description.

" The liberality shewn in first opening the door of St. Paul's to the monument of Mr. Howard, who was a Dissenter, already gives the assurance, that difference of religion will not deter from doing honour to striking worth, without regard to the persuasion of those who may afford examples of it. All partaking in the good which they may have done, all are bound to acknowledge and encourage it.

" Upon the same reasoning, some spot might be reserved for eminent foreigners, who are very properly, upon principles of the same general kind, while living, associated to the Royal Society and other learned bodies.

" But none ought to be admitted in consequence of the with or sole opinion of families or individuals.

" It

"It might, perhaps, be thought proper to
leave it to the Royal Academy to form a
general plan; and they might clafs the feveral defcriptions, allotting places to each.

"It is furely of fome confequence to whom
the firft monument in St. Paul's fhould be
erected; and who can be fo proper to begin this felection as Mr. Howard? He
fpent his life and fortune in fervices which
were highly dangerous to himfelf, but beneficial to every country and every age.
Though engaged in doing the moft active
good, he created no enemies, and excited
no envy, even in his life-time; the purity
of his intentions leaving him fuperior to all
purfuits of vanity or ambition. His merits
were of fuch a general and fundamental
nature, as to ferve for an example to all
ranks, profeffions, and nations.

"It belongs to the Committee to determine, whether there is any thing in thefe
reflections which can contribute to do that
real juftice to his memory which it deferves.
" L."

SAMUEL

SAMUEL JOHNSON, LL. D.

was of opinion that the happiest as well as the most virtuous persons were to be found amongst those who united with a business or profession a love of literature.

He was constantly earnest with his friends when they had thoughts of marriage, to look out for a religious wife*. " A principle of
" honour, or fear of the world," added he,
" will many times keep a man in decent order;
" but when a woman loses her religion she in
" general loses the only tie that will restrain
" her actions. Plautus in his Amphytrio
" makes Alcmena say beautifully to her hus-
" band :

---

* An able and excellent instructor of youth in Berkshire has (as he tells his friends) universally observed, that unless in early life boys have serious impressions of religion they seldom or ever turn out well when they come into the world. He tells with pleasure, that one of his pupils had behaved in a brutal manner to one of the ushers; but having occasion some time afterwards to undergo a religious examination previous to his taking the sacrament, he of his own accord visited the usher, and in terms of the greatest contrition and humility asked his pardon, and assured him that he would never give him any offence again.

Non ego illam mihi dotem duco esse, quæ dos dicitur,
Sed pudicitiam, et pudorem, et sedatum cupidinem,
Deûm metum, parentum amorum, et cognatum concordiam.
Tibi morigera, atque ut munifica sim bonis, prosim probis.

He was one day asked by Mr. Cator, what the Opposition meant by their flaming speeches and violent pamphlets against Lord North's administration. "They mean, Sir, rebellion," said he; "they mean in spite to destroy that "country which they are not permitted to "govern."

Mrs. Cotterell having one day asked him to introduce her to a celebrated writer, "Dear- "est Madam," said he, "you had better let "it alone; the best part of every author is in "general to be found in his book, I assure "you." This opinion he has dilated with his usual perspicuity, and illustrated by one of the most appropriate and excellent similies in the English language *.

---

* " A transition from an author's book to his conversa- " tion is too often like an entrance into a large city after a " distant prospect: remotely we see nothing but spires of " temples and turrets of palaces, and imagine it the resi- " dence of splendour, grandeur, and magnificence; but " when we have passed the gates we find it perplexed with " narrow passages, disgraced with despicable cottages, em- " barrassed with obstructions, and clouded with smoke."— *Rambler,* No. 14.

On being asked in his last illness, what physician he had sent for—"Dr. Heberden," replied he, "*ultimum Romanorum*, the last of the learned physicians *".

The learned and excellent Mr. Charles Cole having once mentioned to him a book lately published on the sacrament, he replied, "Sir, I look upon the sacrament as the palladium of religion: I hope that no prophane hands will venture to touch it."

To his friend Dr. Burney he said a few hours before he died, taking the Doctor's hands within his, and casting his eyes towards Heaven with a look of the most fervent piety: "My dear friend, while you live do all the good you can."

The following Letter of Dr. Johnson to the son of an old and learned friend of his on his taking orders, should be put into the hands of every young man destined to that holy profession:

* Dr. Johnson was not acquainted with that elegant scholar, Sir George Baker, late President of the College of Physicians.

"DEAR

" Dear Sir,

" Not many days ago Dr. L. shewed me a
" letter in which you make kind mention of
" me; I hope, therefore, you will not be dis-
" pleased that I endeavour to preserve your
" good will by some observations which your
" letter suggested to me.

" You are afraid of falling into some im-
" proprieties in the daily service by reading
" to an audience that requires no exactness.
" Your fear, I hope, secures you from danger.
" They who contract absurd habits are such
" as have no fear. It is impossible to do the
" same thing very often without some pecu-
" liarity of manner; but that manner may
" be good or bad, and a little care will at
" least preserve it from being bad: to make it
" very good, there must, I think, be some-
" thing of natural or casual felicity which
" cannot be taught. Your present method of
" making your sermons seems very judicious;
" few frequent preachers can be supposed to
" have sermons more their own than yours
" will be. Take care to register somewhere
" or other the authors from whom your se-
" veral discourses are borrowed; and do not
" imagine that you shall always remember
" even

" even what perhaps you now think it impof-
" fible to forget.

" My advice, however, is, that you attempt
" from time to time an original fermon, and in
" the labour of compofition do not burden your
" mind with too much at once; do not exact
" from yourfelf at one effort of excogitation
" propriety of thought and elegance of ex-
" preffion. Invent firft, and then embellifh.
" The production of fomething where nothing
" was before, is an act of greater energy than
" the expanfion or decoration of the thing
" produced. Set down diligently your thoughts
" as they rife, in the firft words that occur,
" and when you have matter you will eafily
" give it form; nor perhaps will this method
" be always neceffary, for by habit your
" thoughts and diction will flow together.

" The compofition of fermons is not very
" difficult; the divifions not only help the
" memory of the hearer, but direct the judg-
" ment of the writer. They fupply fources
" of invention, and keep every part in its
" proper place. What I like leaft in your
" letter is your account of the manners of
" the parifh, from which I gather that it has
" been long neglected by the parfon. The
" Dean

" Dean of Carlisle (now Bishop of Dromore),
" who was then a little rector in Northamp-
" tonshire, told me, that it might be discerned
" whether or no there was a clergyman re-
" sident in a parish, by the civil or savage
" manners of the people. Such a congre-
" gation as yours stand in much need of re-
" formation; and I would not have you think
" it impossible to reform them. A very savage
" parish was civilized by a decayed gentle-
" woman, who came among them to teach a
" petty school. My learned friend, Dr.
" Wheeler, of Oxford, when he was a young
" man, had the care of a neighbouring parish
" for fifteen pounds a year, which he was
" never paid; but he counted it a conve-
" nience that it compelled him to make a
" sermon weekly. One woman he could not
" bring to the communion, and when he re-
" proved or exhorted her, she only answered
" she was no scholar. He was advised to set
" some good woman or man of the parish, a
" little wiser than herself, to talk to her in
" language level to her mind. Such honest,
" I may call them holy artifices, must be
" practised by every clergyman; for all means
" must be tried by which souls may be saved.
" Talk to your people, however, as much as
" you can; and you will find that the more
                            " frequently

"frequently you converse with them upon
"religious subjects, the more willingly they
"will attend, and the more submissively they
"will learn. A clergyman's diligence always
"makes him venerable. I think I have now
"only to say, that in the momentous work
"that you have undertaken I pray God to
"bless you.

"I am, Sir,

"Your most humble servant,

"SAM. JOHNSON."

Bolt Court, Aug. 30, 1780.

The pen of the poet and of the orator has often been employed in describing the miseries of war; but have the horrors of that hideous scourge of the human race been ever depicted with greater strength of language and power of description than by this sublime and impressive writer?

"It is wonderful," says Dr. Johnson, "with
"what coolness and indifference the greater
"part of mankind see war commence. Those
"that hear of it at a distance, or read of it
"in books, but have never presented its evils
"to their minds, consider it as little more than
"a splendid game; a proclamation, an army,
                    "a battle,

"a battle, and a triumph. Some indeed
"must perish in the most successful field;
"but they die upon the bed of honour, re-
"sign *their lives amidst the joys of conquest, and,
"filled with England's glory, smile in death.*

"The life of a modern soldier," continues
he, "is but ill represented by heroic fiction.
"War has means of destruction more formi-
"dable than the cannon and the sword. Of
"the thousands and ten thousands that pe-
"rished in our late contests with France and
"Spain, a very small part ever felt the stroke
"of the enemy; the rest languished in tents
"and in ships, amidst damps and putrefac-
"tion; pale, torpid, spiritless, and helpless,
"gasping and groaning, unpitied amongst
"men made obdurate by long continuance of
"hopeless pity, and were at last whelmed in
"pits, or heaved into the ocean without no-
"tice and without remembrance. By incom-
"modious encampments and unwholesome
"stations, where courage is useless and en-
"terprise impracticable, fleets are silently
"dispeopled, and armies sluggishly melted
"away. Thus is a people gradually exhausted,
"for the most part, with little effect. The
"wars of civilized nations make very few
"changes in the system of empire. The
"public

" public perceives scarcely any alteration but
" an increase of debt; and the few individuals
" who are benefited have not the clearest right
" to their advantages. If he that shared the
" danger enjoyed the profit, and, after bleed-
" ing in the battle, grew rich by the victory,
" he might shew his gains without envy;
" but, at the conclusion of a ten years war,
" how are we recompensed for the death of
" multitudes * and the expence of millions,
" but by contemplating the sudden glories of
" paymasters and agents, contractors and
" commissaries, whose equipages shine like

---

* Fifteen millions of Americans were put to death in the space of forty years after the discovery of America; and by the confession of Philip the Second, King of Spain, he was the occasion of the death of five millions more! Mr. Scott, of Amwell, says pathetically on the miseries of war:

" I hate that drum's discordant sound,
" Parading round, and round, and round;
" To thoughtless youth it pleasure yields,
" And lures from cities and from fields:
" To me it talks of ravag'd plains,
" And burning towns, and ruin'd swains,
" And mangl'd limbs and dying groans,
" And widows tears and orphans moans,
" And all that misery's hand bestows
" To fill the catalogue of human woes."

" meteors,

" meteors, and whose palaces rise like exha-
" lations?"

Johnson's 'Lives of the Poets' have been found fault with on account of certain minute details of the weaknesses of some of the persons which they commemorate. He said, in defence of this, " that, as a biographer, he
" was bound to describe the person as he really
" was, and not to terrify or to render mankind
" desperate, by holding out models of abso-
" lute and unattainable perfection to their
" imitation." Johnson's works will remain as long as the language, of which he has fixed the basis, shall remain; and, whatever mistakes with respect to etymology, and a knowledge of the northern tongues, his Dictionary may contain, they are in general those of Junius and Skynner, of persons who had made those languages their peculiar study. With respect to his moral writings, it will ever be said, in honour of the purity of them, with the elegant Mrs. Montague, " an angel
" himself could never have denied an *impri-*
" *matur* to any of them."

" Dr. Johnson addressed the following ele-
" gant letter to Mr. Hastings.

" To

" To the Honourable WARREN HASTINGS,
" Governor General of Bengal, &c. &c.

" Amidſt the importance and multiplicity
" of affairs in which your great offices engage
" you, I take the liberty of recalling your
" attention for a moment to literature, and
" will not prolong the interruption by an apo-
" logy which your character makes needleſs.

" Mr. Hoole, a gentleman long known and
" long eſteemed in the India Houſe, after
" having tranſlated Taſſo, has undertaken
" Arioſto. How well he is qualified for his
" undertaking he has already ſhewn. He is
" deſirous of your favour in promoting his
" propoſals, and flatters me by ſuppoſing that
" my teſtimony may advance his intereſt.

" It is a new thing for a Clerk of the India
" Houſe to tranſlate poets; it is a new thing
" for a Governor of Bengal to patronize learn-
" ing. That he may find his ingenuity re-
" warded, and that learning may flouriſh
" under your protection, is the wiſh of,

    " Sir,

     " Your moſt humble ſervant,
" Jan. 1781.   " SAMUEL JOHNSON."

WARREN HASTINGS, ESQ.

GOVERNOR GENERAL OF INDIA.

For the following Memoirs of Mr. Hastings the Compiler is indebted to Major John Scott, the strenuous and grateful * friend of that distinguished person.

Mr. Hastings was born in the year 1732-3, and descended from a family of great respectability, which for many centuries had possessed considerable estates in the counties of Worcester and Gloucester.

The Father of Mr. Hastings was a Clergyman, and held the living of Churchill, in Gloucestershire, a village near Daylesford. On his decease Mr. Hastings was removed by his uncle Mr. Howard Hastings to Westminster School, where he was educated, and went into College the head of his election in the year 1746. His acquaintance with the first Lord Mansfield commenced while he was at West-

---

* Mr. Hastings has so completely the talent of attaching persons to him, in common with many other excellent qualities of Julius Cæsar, that his friends may swear with those of the Roman Emperor, *Ita ipso vivente vivam, ita ipso moriente moriar.*

minster

minster School, and at a time when the former was Attorney General: Lord Mansfield, through life, professed the strongest friendship for him, and the highest opinion of his talents and public services.

On the decease of his uncle Howard Hastings, whose fortune was inconsiderable, compared to the general idea of its amount, young Warren Hastings was to determine on his future situation. Doctor Nichols, the Head Master of Westminster School, had ever treated him with the greatest kindness, and, on so unexpected a turn in his fortune, offered to be himself at the whole expence of completing his education at Oxford. Mr. Creswick, an India Director, and executor of his uncle, offered him a writer's appointment to Bengal. Fortunately for his country, Mr. Hastings chose the latter, embarked for Bengal in the winter of 1749, and arrived in Calcutta in the summer of 1750. The English at that time were mere merchants, and Calcutta an inconsiderable commercial town. They had factories also in different parts of Bengal for the purpose of providing an annual investment for the East India Company, which was principally purchased by bullion sent from England. To one of these factories Mr. Hastings was soon

soon appointed, and from thence detached into the interior parts of Bengal, where, in a seclusion from the society of his countrymen, he acquired a knowledge of the Persian language which few then possessed, though his example has since been so generally followed, that it is now critically understood by almost every civil servant of the Company, and by many of their officers in the army.

At the capture of Calcutta by the Nabob Surajah Doulah in 1756, orders were issued for the seizure of every Englishman in Bengal, and Mr. Hastings was brought a prisoner to Moorshadabad, the capital; but being well known to many men of rank at the Nabob's court, he was treated with indulgence, and allowed to reside at the Dutch factory of Calcapore. When the fleet and army under Watson and Clive arrived in the river of Bengal, Mr. Hastings joined Colonel Clive, and served as a volunteer at the re-capture of Calcutta, and at the night attack of the Nabob's camp. He then resumed his civil appointments; and, after the deposition of the Nabob Surajah Doulah, became the British Minister at the court of his successor. This office he filled with great credit to himself, and advantage to the public, until the year

year 1761, when he became a Member of the Government. In February 1765 he quitted Bengal with his friend Mr. Vanfittart; his fortune did not, as was fuppofed, exceed thirty thoufand pounds, the principal part of which he left behind him, and, his remittances failing, he was early compelled to apply for leave to return to Bengal. His friends, however, had then little influence in the direction, and his application was unfuccefsful. In the year 1766, Mr. Haftings, by the advice of Doctor Johnfon, propofed the inftitution of a Profefforfhip for the ftudy of the Perfian Language at Oxford, and might have been at the head of that inftitution at this moment, if, fortunately for his country, a change in the politics of Leadenhall Street had not taken place. In the winter of 1766 the affairs of the Eaft India Company were brought before Parliament, and Mr. Haftings was examined for feveral hours at the bar of the Houfe of Commons, where the information which he gave was fo clear and fatisfactory, that it brought him into general notice.

A change in the next year took place in Leadenhall Street, and he was appointed fecond member of the adminiftration at Madras, and to fucceed to the government. He left England

Egland in the winter of 1768, and remained at Mad as n'il January 1772, when he proceeded to Bengal, being appointed by the Company to fill that government, and with unlimited powers. This appointment he received very unexpectedly, and without folicitation on his part. The circumstances which led to it properly make a part of his history.

In the year 1765, the Company obtained the sovereignty of Bengal, which Lord Clive had assured them would yield, after the payment of every possible expence, a clear profit of a million *per annum:* the consequence of this representation was, that their stock rose to double its former value, and the King's ministers claimed a right to Bengal for the nation. To prevent the agitation of this question of right, the Company agreed to pay five hundred thousand pounds a year to government, and they increased their dividend from eight to twelve and a half *per cent.* A very short time proved the fallacy of Lord Clive's statement; for, between the years 1765 and 1771, the resources of Bengal barely balanced its public expenditure. Bills were drawn by Bengal upon England for twelve hundred thousand pounds, and a debt to that amount was contracted abroad.

The

The Company did not impute their difappointment to a want of ability in Bengal to yield a million furplus, but to the defective fyftem which Lord Clive had eftablifhed, whofe principle it was to leave the collection of the revenues, and the adminiftration of juftice, in the hands of a native minifter; they determined, therefore, to try a new experiment: they difplaced the native minifter, and left it to the Britifh government of Bengal to form a new fyftem, to be directed by their own adminiftration.

At the head of this adminiftration, and with unlimited authority, they placed Mr. Haftings: and the man who was rejected in 1766, when he applied to return upon any terms to Bengal, who was reduced by their refufal to propofe the inftitution of a profefforfhip at Oxford as a plan for adding to his means of fubfiftence, was, without any folicitation of his own, appointed to fill the higheft office which a Britifh fubject could poffefs.

In April 1772 Mr. Haftings affumed the government of Bengal, and for two years was feduloufly employed in forming and carrying into effect thofe plans and regulations under which

which Bengal has for six-and-twenty years enjoyed internal tranquillity, the natives private security and happiness, and the British nation the greatest public advantages. In this period, he regulated the collection of the public revenues, and the administration of civil and criminal justice. He formed foreign alliances, which added to the security and the wealth of Bengal. He opened a communication with Egypt by the Red Sea, which promised the greatest advantages to Bengal, and would have fixed the British influence in Egypt on a foundation not to be shaken by any efforts which France might now make, if the short-sighted policy of the Company had not counteracted his measures in this instance, under an idea that a commercial intercourse with Turkey through Egypt might affect the trade of London. He deputed a public minister to Thibet, and kept up a friendly intercourse with the Lama, which has continued uninterruptedly to the present time. It is but bare justice to Mr. Hastings to say, that every thing of domestic regulation or foreign connection, by which Bengal has so eminently flourished, originated in the measures which he himself adopted in the first year of his administration.

While

While Mr. Haſtings was laboriouſly exerting himſelf for the public ſervice in Bengal, a rigid enquiry into the paſt conduct of the Company's ſervants was carried on in the Houſe of Commons. Violent (and in moſt inſtances very unjuſt) cenſures were caſt upon them; but no part of this general cenſure reſted upon Mr. Haſtings, whoſe reputation roſe ſtill higher from the ſcrutiny. The reſult was, that the Miniſter, Lord North, propoſed to fix a new government for Bengal, and that the members ſhould be nominated by parliament. He pronounced a very warm panegyrick on the character and conduct of Mr. Haſtings, who was nominated Governor General of Bengal for five years, with the unanimous conſent of both Houſes.

It would be invidious, and would make no proper part of the preſent Biographical Sketch, to enter into the diſſentions which prevailed in Bengal under the new ſyſtem, and which continued with little intermiſſion until Mr. Francis quitted it in 1780. It can however with truth be aſſerted, that thoſe diſſentions did not diſturb the public tranquillity. The regulations adopted by Mr. Haſtings on his ſucceeding to the government in 1772 produced all the effects which he had predicted ed from them: the public debt was paid off, and Bengal yielded a tribute of more than a million a year to Great Britain, until meafures originating in England again involved us in difficulties in India.

The American War excited the reftlefs ambition of France. She early determined on an interference, nor had fhe beheld without jealoufy the rife, progrefs, and great improvement of our Indian Empire. Her great object was, to annihilate our power. To effect this, fhe commenced her intrigues in India long before fhe threw off the mafk in Europe. The fleet, commanded by D'Eftaing, which failed for America in April 1778, was originally deftined for India, though, by the prefsing folicitations of Dr. Franklin, its deftination was fubfequently changed. In the fucceeding years of the war, France fent twenty fail of the line, feven thoufand land forces, and feven millions fterling to India. We had alfo to contend with Hyder Ally Cawn and the Mahrattas. During the whole of this arduous conteft, Mr. Haftings remained at the head of the Bengal government—peace was concluded with all our enemies—we loft no territory: on the contrary, by reftoring the conquefts made from France and Holland

Holland in India, Lord Lanfdown recovered two Weft India Iflands to Great Britain.

Were we not writing at a period when the events are freſh in our recollection, it could hardly be credited, that the Houfe of Commons, during the moſt critical period of the war, voted the recal of Mr. Haſtings—a vote which the better fenfe of the Company refiſted; and for fo doing, at a fubfequent period, the Member (Mr. Dundas) who moved the recal declared that the Company deferved the thanks of the public.

Mr. Haſtings was exprefsly defired by the Company to retain the government until peace was completely reſtored in India. He did fo, and on the return of tranquiility, applied for the appointment of a fucceſſor, and notified his intention to return to England.

The meaſures which were at that time purſued in England prevented the Company from appointing a fucceſſor to Mr. Haſtings. In November 1783 Mr. Fox propofed his celebrated India bill. It was rejected by the Houfe of Lords, and his adminiſtration difmiſſed. Under the new miniſtry, a fyſtem was framed for the government of India.

Full

Full juftice was done to the merits of Mr. Haftings—thanks were tranfmitted to him for his long, faithful, and able fervices by the Company; and in compliance with his requeft a fucceffor was appointed.

In June 1785, Mr. Haftings arrived in England, and was received with every mark of attention by his Sovereign, the Minifters, and the Eaft India Company. The Directors repeated their thanks to him unanimoufly for his long, faithful, and valuable fervices. On leaving Bengal, public addreffes were prefented to him by the Britifh fubjects of Calcutta, regretting his departure, and ftating in ftrong terms his beneficial exertions in the public fervice. Similar addreffes were tranfmitted to him from the army, and he appears to have been held in univerfal veneration by the natives of India.

If there ever was a man whofe life had been fpent in the fervice of the public, that might look to an undifturbed enjoyment of *otium cum dignitate* for the remnant of his days, furely Mr. Haftings was that man. He had been thirteen years the Governor or Governor General of Bengal; the firft under the Company's appointments, the latter by five feparate parliamentary appointments. He recovered that government, loaded with a heavy public debt contracted in peace, and its resources not exceeding three millions sterling a year, a sum barely adequate to its annual expences. He quitted it, after a long, arduous, and succesful war, with its empire considerably extended, with the general voice of his countrymen and the natives in his favour, and its annual resources five millions and a half sterling, being two millions beyond the annual expenditure. Mark the contrast at home! When his government commenced in 1772, the empire of Great Britain extended over America—her debt was one hundred and thirty millions. In 1785 she had lost America, some of her West India Islands, Minorca, and her debt was two hundred and sixty millions. It was broadly stated by Mr. Dundas, and not denied, that Bengal had been in a progressive state of improvement under the British government. Facts of public notoriety proved the truth of this assertion; but what individual unsupported merit can resist the fury of Party? On the day Mr. Hastings arrived in London, Mr. Burke notified to the House of Commons, that early in the next sessions he would move an enquiry into the conduct M. Hastings

During

During the recess, Mr. Hastings was strenuously advised by men who well knew the nature of Parliament to pay no attention to this menace; or, if he was determined to notice it, to come into Parliament himself, and a seat was offered to him. He rejected the advice in both instances, declaring that he neither wished to court nor to elude the enquiry, still less was he disposed to owe his security to the forbearance of Mr. Burke; he, therefore, expressly desired Major Scott to ask Mr. Burke in his place at the next meeting of parliament, whether he meant to institute the enquiry or not? To this question Mr. Burke gave an evasive answer, but Mr. Fox a direct one. Subsequent to this conversation in the House, a general meeting of the Party in opposition assembled at Burlington House. The question was debated, and great difference of opinion prevailed. The late Lord North, the present Marquis of Hertford, the Duke of Norfolk, then Lord Surry, and many other gentlemen, were against any further proceedings; but Mr. Fox, with an unjustifiable generosity, for which he has been amply repaid, supported Mr. Burke, and, conceiving his character to be at stake, strenuously contended for the proceeding, and it was taken up as a party measure. Mr. Dempster,

Dempster, the late Colonel Cathcart, Mr. Sloper, Mr. Nichols, and a few other members, seceded; but the party in general went with Mr. Fox. Two years were spent in the House of Commons before the impeachment was voted. The trial lasted six years in Westminster Hall, and a seventh in the chamber of Parliament: so that if we reckon from 1785, when Mr. Burke gave his notice, to 1795, when the acquittal was pronounced, this celebrated trial might vie for duration with the siege of Troy*.

The evidence on this celebrated trial was summed up by Lord Thurlow with an accuracy and precision that reflect the highest honour on that distinguished character; and his speeches contain the best history of Mr. Hastings's administration that has hitherto been published †.

This remarkable prosecution cost the nation above one hundred thousand pounds, and the law expences of Mr. Hastings amounted to more

---

* *Quam neque Tydides, nec Larissæus Achilles,*
Non anni domuere decem, non mille loquelæ.

VIRGIL.

† They are to be found in Debrett's Lords Debates for February, March, and April 1795.

than

than sixty thousand pounds; to which, if we add the incidental expences attending it, we may fairly say, that the trial cost him one hundred thousand pounds also. While it was depending, it had been repeatedly said in the House, that in the event of his acquittal he had an undoubted right to remuneration from parliament. A petition was accordingly drawn up by him, but the Minister would not advise his Majesty to agree to its being presented. A general court was afterwards called at the India House, and a motion made by Mr. Alderman Lushington, prefaced by a very eloquent and energetic speech in favour of Mr. Hastings. After the fullest acknowledgment of his services, it was proposed to pay the legal expences of his trial, and to grant him a pension of five thousand pounds a year for the remainder of the charter. Both motions were carried by considerable majorities; but doubts were started as to the right of the Company to dispose of their own money without the consent of the Board of Commissioners. The great lawyers held different opinions; but the attorney and solicitor general were decidedly against such a right being vested in the Company. On this decision a new motion was brought forward in concert with his Majesty's Ministers, who

agreed

agreed (without any reference to the trial), in confideration of Mr. Haftings's public services, to grant him a penfion of four thoufand pounds a year for twenty-eight years and a half; of this penfion they immediately gave him forty-two thoufand pounds, and lent him in addition fifty thoufand pounds. The whole fum voted was one hundred and fourteen thoufand pounds, of which they immediately paid him ninety-two thoufand; the remainder he was to receive at the rate of five thoufand pounds a year to the clofe of the charter; the other two thoufand pounds were to be ftopped to repay the loan of fifty thoufand pounds, and his eftate was charged with a mortgage for the fum of fourteen thoufand pounds, which would be due to the Company when the charter expired. We have given this account, becaufe few have known what fum was really granted to Mr. Haftings.

There have been various impeachments at different periods of our Hiftory; but Mr. Haftings is the firft Britifh fubject acquitted after a trial on an accufation preferred by the Commons. There are many inftances of acquittal at the bar of the Houfe of Lords; but in all others they have proceeded from a difference

ference between the two Houses, as in the cases of the Whig Lords in the reign of William the Third, and of Lord Oxford in the reign of George the First, and sometimes by the Commons not prosecuting. But to the honour of the administration of justice in this reign, the trial of Mr. Hastings was brought to a legal determination without any interference on the part of the Crown, the King's Ministers, or the House of Commons, and by those Lords only who had generally attended the trial. Two other circumstances highly honourable to Mr. Hastings ought also to be mentioned. He was impeached in the name of the people of England, for acts of tyranny, injustice, and oppression exercised upon the natives of India. While the trial was yet pending, the natives of India, of all ranks and sects, transmitted to the East India Company, through Lord Cornwallis, their full disavowal of the charge, and expressed their perfect satisfaction with the conduct of Mr. Hastings, and their strong attachment to him. When the intelligence of his acquittal arrived in India, it was received with enthusiastic pleasure. Addresses of congratulation were transmitted to him by the British subjects in Calcutta, by the officers of the army, and by all classes amongst the natives:

natives: and the event was celebrated by public rejoicings in every part of Bengal.

The charge preferred againſt him in behalf of the Eaſt India Company was alſo diſclaimed by that body. He was accuſed of having brought upon them great loſs and damage, and of having wantonly waſted their property. Men bred to buſineſs reſorted to the evidence of figures; they found that Mr. Haſtings had preſerved the Britiſh Empire in India entire, had even improved it during a hazardous war, and had added two millions a year to their annual reſources. They thought him entitled to applauſe rather than to cenſure, and they returned him their unanimous thanks for his long, faithful, and able ſervices.

Prejudice has now ſubſided, and England and India proclaim with united rapture their obligations to Mr. Haſtings.

In private life, he is univerſally allowed to be a man of very general knowledge—an excellent Engineer (having practiſed that art under the celebrated Mr. Robins), and an Architect. His Minutes on military ſubjects prove him well qualified to command an army; and that he is an able Financier, and an admirable

rable Lawyer, appears by his 'Plans for the Better Adminiſtration of Juſtice,' which have been publiſhed.

Many ſcholars and men of talents have tranſlated the celebrated Ode of Horace which begins, " Otium divos rogat, &c." The tranſlation of Mr. Haſtings is ſuperior to them all. He wrote the following lines in Mr. Mickle's excellent Verſion of the Luſiad of Camoëns, to be inſerted at the end of the ſpeech of Pacheco:

" Yet ſhrink not, gallant Luſiad, nor repine
" That Man's eternal deſtiny is thine;
" Whene'er ſucceſs the advent'rous chief befriends,
" Fell Malice on his parting ſteps attends;
" On Britain's candidates for fame await,
" As now on thee, the harſh decrees of Fate;
" Thus are Ambition's fondeſt hopes o'erreach'd,
" One dies impriſon'd, and one lives impeach'd."

The ENGRAVING of Mr. HASTINGS which accompanies theſe Memoirs is taken from a Buſt made by that claſſical Sculptor Mr. Banks, of Newman-ſtreet. It reſembles very much the head of Aratus, the founder of the celebrated Achæan League, in the Ludoviſi Gardens at Rome.

RICHARD WARREN, M.D.

This celebrated physician being asked one day what was the best school of physic, replied, "The best school of physic that I know is "a large London hospital *." Lord Mansfield said of Lord Chancellor Hardwicke, that Wisdom herself would have chosen to speak by his mouth: Sagacity itself would have chosen that of Dr. Warren to record its observations; his expressions were neat and forcible, and plainly evinced that they arose from a mind pregnant with information and acuteness. Of every subject on which he conversed he always went to the leading feature, the discriminating trait; and left every hearer convinced, that, had he pursued the Law, had he studied Theology, or had he taken to Politics, he would have been as distinguished in them as he was in his own particular science. In this he verified what was said of the illustrious Marshal Catinat to Louis XIV. " Does your Majesty want an

---

* This however, like every other aphorism, must be understood with allowance. The great physician who made it supposed that a certain portion of medical reading and lectures had been gone through before the student observed the practice of that useful and arduous science.

" arch-

"archbishop, a chancellor, a general, or a prime minister? You may take Catinat for any of those great situations; he will fill either of them with honour to you and to himself."

DR. LANCASTER

was the author of a very elegant Essay on Delicacy, printed in Dodsley's Collection of Prose Pieces, in two volumes, 12mo.

He says in a MS. letter to the Rev. Dr. Charlett:—" I never heard English printers blamed so much for any thing, as for their papers being too white. I have found by experience, that eyes are very good things; and yet I will not say that I found it out first, for they say old Friar Bacon knew it, and even some Antediluvians lived long enough to discover it. Now brown paper preserves the eye better than white, and for that reason the wise Chinese write upon brown. So the Ægyptians, so Aldus and Stephens printed, and on such paper or vellum are old MSS. written; and when authors and readers agree to be wiser, we shall avoid printing on a *glaring white paper* *."

* The completest specimen of excellent typography in every respect is the Louvre Thomas à Kempis, folio.

FINIS.

ADDENDA.

To the Article *BEAUMELLE.*

Note.

"In all political contests," says Aristotle in his Politics, "the contending parties alternately appeal to justice; but the one party measures justice by an arithmetical, and the other by a geometrical standard: whereas in fact it ought to be regulated by both; and such governments as equitably combine arithmetical and geometrical proportion together into one compound political ratio can alone expect to be prosperous or stable." See the excellent Translation of the Works of Aristotle, by John Gillies, LL. D. Vol. II. p. 335.

Who that understands the British constitution does not see in this sentence of Aristotle a complete description of its peculiar excellence?

To the Article *GEORGE THE SECOND.*

Note on the word "Metropolis."

"The King said in Council, that the Magistrates had not done their duty, but that he would do his own; and a Proclamation was published, directing us to keep our servants within doors, as the peace was now to be preserved by force. The soldiers were sent out to different parts, and the town is now quiet."

Dr. Johnson to Mrs. Thrale, London, June 9, 1780.

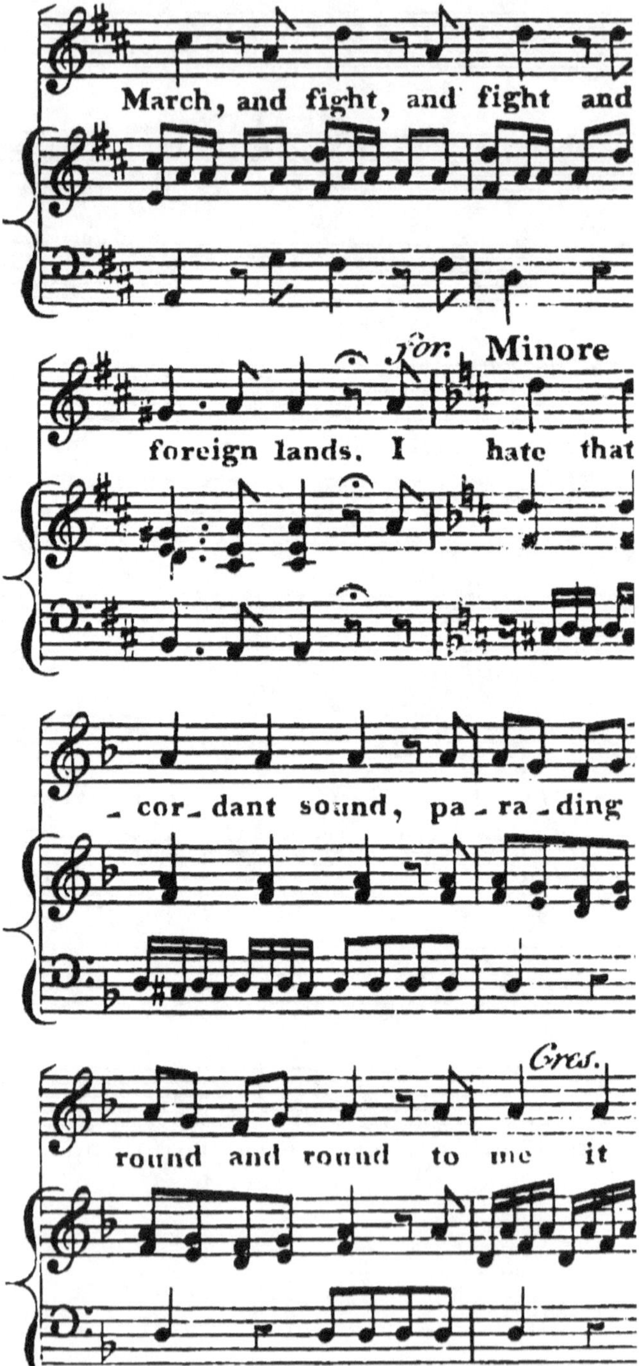
March, and fight, and fight and
for:
Minore
foreign lands. I hate that
- cor - dant sound, pa - ra - ding
Cres.
round and round to me it

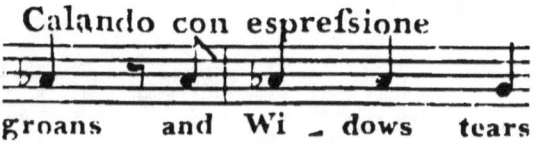

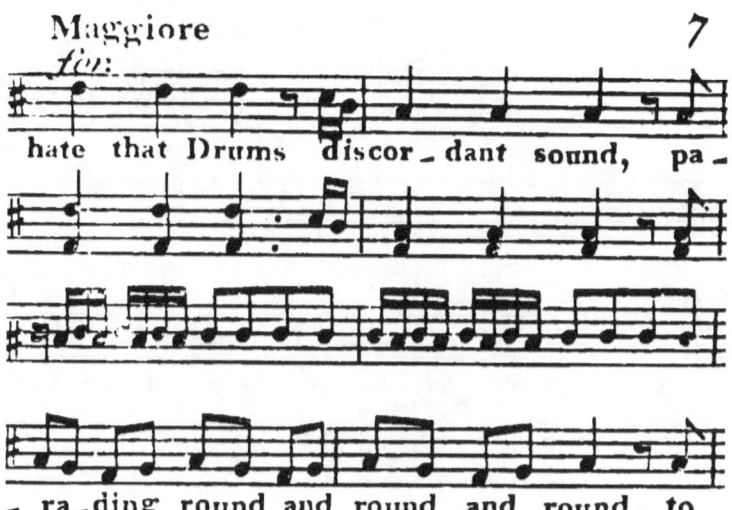

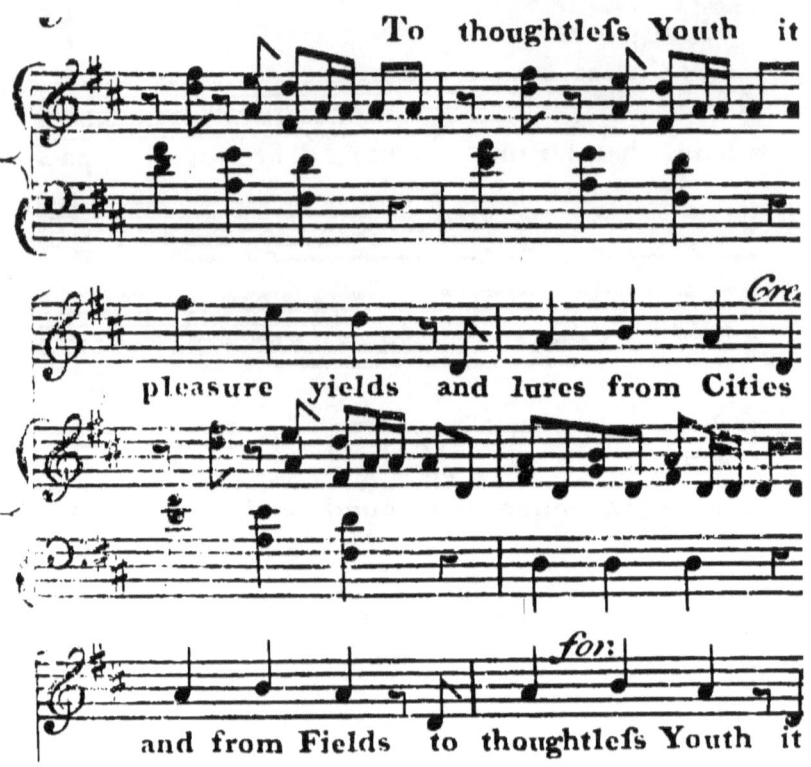

www.ingramcontent.com/pod-product-compliance
Lightning Source LLC
Chambersburg PA
CBHW031846220426
43663CB00006B/511